THE PELICAN SHAKESPEARE
GENERAL EDITORS

STEPHEN ORGEL
A. R. BRAUNMULLER

The Third Part of Henry the Sixth

The murder of King Henry by Richard of Gloucester (V.6),
frontispiece to the play in Nicholas Rowe's Shakespeare,
1709, the first illustrated edition. The play was performed
throughout the Restoration in an adaptation by John Crowne
called *The Miseries of Civil War*. The costumes are a mixture
of medieval and modern, the setting gothic, the decor
eighteenth-century, all reflecting stage practice.

William Shakespeare

The Third Part of
Henry the Sixth

EDITED BY WILLIAM MONTGOMERY
WITH AN INTRODUCTION BY JANIS LULL

PENGUIN BOOKS

PENGUIN BOOKS
Published by the Penguin Group
Penguin Group (USA) Inc., 375 Hudson Street, New York, New York 10014, U.S.A.
Penguin Group (Canada), 90 Eglinton Avenue East, Suite 700, Toronto, Ontario,
Canada M4P 2Y3 (a division of Pearson Penguin Canada Inc.)
Penguin Books Ltd, 80 Strand, London WC2R 0RL, England
Penguin Ireland, 25 St Stephen's Green, Dublin 2, Ireland (a division of Penguin Books Ltd)
Penguin Group (Australia), 250 Camberwell Road, Camberwell, Victoria 3124,
Australia (a division of Pearson Australia Group Pty Ltd)
Penguin Books India Pvt Ltd, 11 Community Centre, Panchsheel Park, New Delhi – 110 017, India
Penguin Group (NZ), 67 Apollo Drive, Mairangi Bay, Auckland 1311, New Zealand
(a division of Pearson New Zealand Ltd)
Penguin Books (South Africa) (Pty) Ltd, 24 Sturdee Avenue, Rosebank, Johannesburg 2196, South Africa

Penguin Books Ltd, Registered Offices: 80 Strand, London WC2R 0RL, England

The Second and Third Parts of King Henry the Sixth edited
by Robert K. Turner, Jr., and George Walton Williams published
in the United States of America in Penguin Books 1967
Revised edition published 1980
This new edition of *The Third Part of Henry the Sixth* edited by
William Montgomery with an introduction by Janis Lull published 2000

9 10 8

Copyright © Penguin Books Inc., 1967
Copyright © Viking Penguin Inc., 1980
Copyright © Penguin Putnam Inc., 2000
All rights reserved

ISBN 978-0-14-071467-8
(CIP data available)

Printed in the United States of America
Set in Adobe Garamond
Designed by Virginia Norey

Contents

Publisher's Note   vi

The Theatrical World   vii

The Texts of Shakespeare   xxiii·

Introduction   xxvii

Genealogical Chart   xl

Note on the Text   xliii

The Third Part of Henry the Sixth   1

Publisher's Note

IT IS ALMOST half a century since the first volumes of the Pelican Shakespeare appeared under the general editorship of Alfred Harbage. The fact that a new edition, rather than simply a revision, has been undertaken reflects the profound changes textual and critical studies of Shakespeare have undergone in the past twenty years. For the new Pelican series, the texts of the plays and poems have been thoroughly revised in accordance with recent scholarship, and in some cases have been entirely reedited. New introductions and notes have been provided in all the volumes. But the new Shakespeare is also designed as a successor to the original series; the previous editions have been taken into account, and the advice of the previous editors has been solicited where it was feasible to do so.

Certain textual features of the new Pelican Shakespeare should be particularly noted. All lines are numbered that contain a word, phrase, or allusion explained in the glossarial notes. In addition, for convenience, every tenth line is also numbered, in italics when no annotation is indicated. The intrusive and often inaccurate place headings inserted by early editors are omitted (as is becoming standard practice), but for the convenience of those who miss them, an indication of locale now appears as the first item in the annotation of each scene.

In the interest of both elegance and utility, each speech prefix is set in a separate line when the speaker's lines are in verse, except when those words form the second half of a verse line. Thus the verse form of the speech is kept visually intact. What is printed as verse and what is printed as prose has, in general, the authority of the original texts. Departures from the original texts in this regard have only the authority of editorial tradition and the judgment of the Pelican editors; and, in a few instances, are admittedly arbitrary.

The Theatrical World

Economic realities determined the theatrical world in which Shakespeare's plays were written, performed, and received. For centuries in England, the primary theatrical tradition was nonprofessional. Craft guilds (or "mysteries") provided religious drama – mystery plays – as part of the celebration of religious and civic festivals, and schools and universities staged classical and neoclassical drama in both Latin and English as part of their curricula. In these forms, drama was established and socially acceptable. Professional theater, in contrast, existed on the margins of society. The acting companies were itinerant; playhouses could be any available space – the great halls of the aristocracy, town squares, civic halls, inn yards, fair booths, or open fields – and income was sporadic, dependent on the passing of the hat or on the bounty of local patrons. The actors, moreover, were considered little better than vagabonds, constantly in danger of arrest or expulsion.

In the late 1560s and 1570s, however, English professional theater began to gain respectability. Wealthy aristocrats fond of drama – the Lord Admiral, for example, or the Lord Chamberlain – took acting companies under their protection so that the players technically became members of their households and were no longer subject to arrest as homeless or masterless men. Permanent theaters were first built at this time as well, allowing the companies to control and charge for entry to their performances.

Shakespeare's livelihood, and the stunning artistic explosion in which he participated, depended on pragmatic and architectural effort. Professional theater requires ways to restrict access to its offerings; if it does not, and admission fees cannot be charged, the actors do not get paid, the costumes go to a pawnbroker, and there is no such thing as a professional, ongoing theatrical tradition. The answer to that economic need arrived in the late 1560s and 1570s with the creation of the so-called public or amphitheater playhouse. Recent discoveries indicate that the precursor of the Globe playhouse in London (where Shakespeare's mature plays were presented) and the Rose theater (which presented Christopher Marlowe's plays and some of Shakespeare's earliest ones) was the Red Lion theater of 1567. Archaeological studies of the foundations of the Rose and Globe theaters have revealed that the open-air theater of the 1590s and later was probably a polygonal building with fourteen to twenty or twenty-four sides, multistoried, from 75 to 100 feet in diameter, with a raised, partly covered "thrust" stage that projected into a group of standing patrons, or "groundlings," and a covered gallery, seating up to 2,500 or more (very crowded) spectators.

These theaters might have been about half full on any given day, though the audiences were larger on holidays or when a play was advertised, as old and new were, through printed playbills posted around London. The metropolitan area's late-Tudor, early-Stuart population (circa 1590–1620) has been estimated at about 150,000 to 250,000. It has been supposed that in the mid-1590s there were about 15,000 spectators per week at the public theaters; thus, as many as 10 percent of the local population went to the theater regularly. Consequently, the theaters' repertories – the plays available for this experienced and frequent audience – had to change often: in the month between September 15 and October 15, 1595, for instance, the Lord Admiral's Men performed twenty-eight times in eighteen different plays.

Since natural light illuminated the amphitheaters' stages, performances began between noon and two o'clock and ran without a break for two or three hours. They often concluded with a jig, a fencing display, or some other nondramatic exhibition. Weather conditions determined the season for the amphitheaters: plays were performed every day (including Sundays, sometimes, to clerical dismay) except during Lent – the forty days before Easter – or periods of plague, or sometimes during the summer months when law courts were not in session and the most affluent members of the audience were not in London.

To a modern theatergoer, an amphitheater stage like that of the Rose or Globe would appear an unfamiliar mixture of plainness and elaborate decoration. Much of the structure was carved or painted, sometimes to imitate marble; elsewhere, as under the canopy projecting over the stage, to represent the stars and the zodiac. Appropriate painted canvas pictures (of Jerusalem, for example, if the play was set in that city) were apparently hung on the wall behind the acting area, and tragedies were accompanied by black hangings, presumably something like crepe festoons or bunting. Although these theaters did not employ what we would call scenery, early modern spectators saw numerous large props, such as the "bar" at which a prisoner stood during a trial, the "mossy bank" where lovers reclined, an arbor for amorous conversation, a chariot, gallows, tables, trees, beds, thrones, writing desks, and so forth. Audiences might learn a scene's location from a sign (reading "Athens," for example) carried across the stage (as in Bertolt Brecht's twentieth-century productions). Equally captivating (and equally irritating to the theater's enemies) were the rich costumes and personal props the actors used: the most valuable items in the surviving theatrical inventories are the swords, gowns, robes, crowns, and other items worn or carried by the performers.

Magic appealed to Shakespeare's audiences as much as it does to us today, and the theater exploited many deceptive and spectacular devices. A winch in the loft above the stage, called "the heavens," could lower and raise actors playing gods, goddesses, and other supernatural figures to and from the main acting area, just as one or more trapdoors permitted entrances and exits to and from the area, called "hell," beneath the stage. Actors wore elementary makeup such as wigs, false beards, and face paint, and they employed pig's bladders filled with animal blood to make wounds seem more real. They had rudimentary but effective ways of pretending to behead or hang a person. Supernumeraries (stagehands or actors not needed in a particular scene) could make thunder sounds (by shaking a metal sheet or rolling an iron ball down a chute) and show lightning (by blowing inflammable resin through tubes into a flame). Elaborate fireworks enhanced the effects of dragons flying through the air or imitated such celestial phenomena as comets, shooting stars, and multiple suns. Horses' hoofbeats, bells (located perhaps in the tower above the stage), trumpets and drums, clocks, cannon shots and gunshots, and the like were common sound effects. And the music of viols, cornets, oboes, and recorders was a regular feature of theatrical performances.

For two relatively brief spans, from the late 1570s to 1590 and from 1599 to 1614, the amphitheaters competed with the so-called private, or indoor, theaters, which originated as, or later represented themselves as, educational institutions training boys as singers for church services and court performances. These indoor theaters had two features that were distinct from the amphitheaters': their personnel and their playing spaces. The amphitheaters' adult companies included both adult men, who played the male roles, and boys, who played the female roles; the private, or indoor, theater companies, on the other hand, were entirely composed of boys aged about 8 to 16, who were, or could pretend to be, candidates for singers in a church or a royal boys' choir. (Until 1660, professional theatrical companies included no women.) The playing space would appear much more familiar to modern audiences than the long-vanished amphitheaters; the later indoor theaters were, in fact, the ancestors of the typical modern theater. They were enclosed spaces, usually rectangular, with the stage filling one end of the rectangle and the audience arrayed in seats or benches across (and sometimes lining) the building's longer axis. These spaces staged plays less frequently than the public theaters (perhaps only once a week) and held far fewer spectators than the amphitheaters: about 200 to 600, as opposed to 2,500 or more. Fewer patrons mean a smaller gross income, unless each pays more. Not surprisingly, then, private theaters charged higher prices than the amphitheaters, probably sixpence, as opposed to a penny for the cheapest entry.

Protected from the weather, the indoor theaters presented plays later in the day than the amphitheaters, and used artificial illumination – candles in sconces or candelabra. But candles melt, and need replacing, snuffing, and trimming, and these practical requirements may have been part of the reason the indoor theaters introduced breaks in the performance, the intermission so dear to the heart of theatergoers and to the pocketbooks of theater concessionaires ever since. Whether motivated by the need to tend to the candles or by the entrepreneurs' wishing to sell oranges and liquor, or both, the indoor theaters eventually established the modern convention of the non-continuous performance. In the early modern "private" theater, musical performances apparently filled the intermissions, which in Stuart theater jargon seem to have been called "acts."

At the end of the first decade of the seventeenth century, the distinction between public amphitheaters and private indoor companies ceased. For various cultural, political, and economic reasons, individual companies gained control of both the public, open-air theaters and the indoor ones, and companies mixing adult men and boys took over the formerly "private" theaters. Despite the death of the boys' companies and of their highly innovative theaters (for which such luminous playwrights as Ben Jonson, George Chapman, and John Marston wrote), their playing spaces and conventions had an immense impact on subsequent plays: not merely for the intervals (which stressed the artistic and architectonic importance of "acts"), but also because they introduced political and social satire as a popular dramatic ingredient, even in tragedy, and a wider range of actorly effects, encouraged by their more intimate playing spaces.

Even the briefest sketch of the Shakespearean theatrical world would be incomplete without some comment on the social and cultural dimensions of theaters and playing in the period. In an intensely hierarchical and status-conscious society, professional actors and their ventures had hardly any respectability; as we have indicated, to protect themselves against laws designed to curb vagabondage and the increase of masterless men, actors resorted to the near-fiction that they were the servants of noble masters, and wore their distinctive livery. Hence the company for which Shakespeare wrote in the 1590s called itself the Lord Chamberlain's Men and pretended that the public, money-getting performances were in fact rehearsals for private performances before that high court official. From 1598, the Privy Council had licensed theatrical companies, and after 1603, with the accession of King James I, the companies gained explicit royal protection, just as the Queen's Men had for a time under Queen Elizabeth. The Chamberlain's Men became the King's Men, and the other companies were patronized by the other members of the royal family.

These designations were legal fictions that half-concealed an important economic and social development, the evolution away from the theater's organization on the model of the guild, a self-regulating confraternity of individual artisans, into a proto-capitalist organization. Shakespeare's company became a joint-stock company, where persons who supplied capital and, in some cases, such as Shakespeare's, capital and talent, employed themselves and others in earning a return on that capital. This development meant that actors and theater companies were outside both the traditional guild structures, which required some form of civic or royal charter, and the feudal household organization of master-and-servant. This anomalous, maverick social and economic condition made theater companies practically unruly and potentially even dangerous; consequently, numerous official bodies – including the London metropolitan and ecclesiastical authorities as well as, occasionally, the royal court itself – tried, without much success, to control and even to disband them.

Public officials had good reason to want to close the theaters: they were attractive nuisances – they drew often riotous crowds, they were always noisy, and they could be politically offensive and socially insubordinate. Until the Civil War, however, anti-theatrical forces failed to shut down professional theater, for many reasons – limited surveillance and few police powers, tensions or outright hostilities among the agencies that sought to check or channel theatrical activity, and lack of clear policies for control. Another reason must have been the theaters' undeniable popularity. Curtailing any activity enjoyed by such a substantial percentage of the population was difficult, as various Roman emperors attempting to limit circuses had learned, and the Tudor-Stuart audience was not merely large, it was socially diverse and included women. The prevalence of public entertainment in this period has been underestimated. In fact, fairs, holidays, games, sporting events, the equivalent of modern parades, freak shows, and street exhibitions all abounded, but the theater was the most widely and frequently available entertainment to which people of every class had access. That fact helps account both for its quantity and for the fear and anger it aroused.

WILLIAM SHAKESPEARE OF
STRATFORD-UPON-AVON, GENTLEMAN

Many people have said that we know very little about William Shakespeare's life – pinheads and postcards are often mentioned as appropriately tiny surfaces on which to record the available information. More imaginatively and perhaps more correctly, Ralph Waldo Emerson wrote, "Shakespeare is the only biographer of Shakespeare. . . . So far from Shakespeare's being the least known, he is the one person in all modern history fully known to us."

In fact, we know more about Shakespeare's life than we do about almost any other English writer's of his era. His last will and testament (dated March 25, 1616) survives, as do numerous legal contracts and court documents involving Shakespeare as principal or witness, and parish records in Stratford and London. Shakespeare appears quite often in official records of King James's royal court, and of course Shakespeare's name appears on numerous title pages and in the written and recorded words of his literary contemporaries Robert Greene, Henry Chettle, Francis Meres, John Davies of Hereford, Ben Jonson, and many others. Indeed, if we make due allowance for the bloating of modern, run-of-the-mill bureaucratic records, more information has survived over the past four hundred years about William Shakespeare of Stratford-upon-Avon, Warwickshire, than is likely to survive in the next four hundred years about any reader of these words.

What we do not have are entire categories of information – Shakespeare's private letters or diaries, drafts and revisions of poems and plays, critical prefaces or essays, commendatory verse for other writers' works, or instructions guiding his fellow actors in their performances, for instance – that we imagine would help us understand and appreciate his surviving writings. For all we know, many such data never existed as written records. Many literary and theatrical critics, not knowing what might once have existed, more or less cheerfully accept the situation; some even make a theoretical virtue of it by claiming that such data are irrelevant to understanding and interpreting the plays and poems.

So, what do we know about William Shakespeare, the man responsible for thirty-seven or perhaps more plays, more than 150 sonnets, two lengthy narrative poems, and some shorter poems?

While many families by the name of Shakespeare (or some variant spelling) can be identified in the English Midlands as far back as the twelfth century, it seems likely that the dramatist's grandfather, Richard, moved to Snitterfield, a town not far from Stratford-upon-Avon, sometime before 1529. In Snitterfield, Richard Shakespeare leased farmland from the very wealthy Robert Arden. By 1552, Richard's son John had moved to a large house on Henley Street in Stratford-upon-Avon, the house that stands today as "The Birthplace." In Stratford, John Shakespeare traded as a glover, dealt in wool, and lent money at interest; he also served in a variety of civic posts, including "High Bailiff," the municipality's equivalent of mayor. In 1557, he married Robert Arden's youngest daughter, Mary. Mary and John had four sons – William was the oldest – and four daughters, of whom only Joan outlived her most celebrated sibling. William was baptized (an event entered in the Stratford parish church records) on April 26, 1564, and it has become customary, without any good factual support, to suppose he was born on April 23, which happens to be the feast day of Saint George, patron saint of England, and is also the date on which he died, in 1616. Shakespeare married Anne Hathaway in 1582, when he was eighteen and she was twenty-six; their first child was born five months later. It has been generally assumed that the marriage was enforced and subsequently unhappy, but these are only assumptions; it has been estimated, for instance, that up to one third of Elizabethan brides were pregnant when they married. Anne and William Shakespeare had three children: Susanna, who married a prominent local physician, John Hall; and the twins Hamnet, who died young in 1596, and Judith, who married Thomas Quiney – apparently a rather shady individual. The name Hamnet was unusual but not unique: he and his twin sister were named for their godparents, Shakespeare's neighbors Hamnet and Judith Sadler. Shakespeare's father died in 1601 (the year of *Hamlet*), and Mary Arden Shakespeare died in 1608 (the year of *Coriolanus*). William Shakespeare's last surviving direct descendant was his granddaughter Elizabeth Hall, who died in 1670.

Between the birth of the twins in 1585 and a clear reference to Shakespeare as a practicing London dramatist in Robert Greene's sensationalizing, satiric pamphlet, *Greene's Groatsworth of Wit* (1592), there is no record of where William Shakespeare was or what he was doing. These seven so-called lost years have been imaginatively filled by scholars and other students of Shakespeare: some think he traveled to Italy, or fought in the Low Countries, or studied law or medicine, or worked as an apprentice actor/writer, and so on to even more fanciful possibilities. Whatever the biographical facts for those "lost" years, Greene's nasty remarks in 1592 testify to professional envy and to the fact that Shakespeare already had a successful career in London. Speaking to his fellow playwrights, Greene warns both generally and specifically:

> ... trust them [actors] not: for there is an upstart crow, beautified with our feathers, that with his tiger's heart wrapped in a player's hide supposes he is as well able to bombast out a blank verse as the best of you; and being an absolute Johannes Factotum, is in his own conceit the only Shake-scene in a country.

The passage mimics a line from *3 Henry VI* (hence the play must have been performed before Greene wrote) and seems to say that "Shake-scene" is both actor and playwright, a jack-of-all-trades. That same year, Henry Chettle protested Greene's remarks in *Kind-Heart's Dream*, and each of the next two years saw the publication of poems – *Venus and Adonis* and *The Rape of Lucrece*, respectively – publicly ascribed to (and dedicated by) Shakespeare. Early in 1595 he was named one of the senior members of a prominent acting company, the Lord Chamberlain's Men, when they received payment for court performances during the 1594 Christmas season.

Clearly, Shakespeare had achieved both success and reputation in London. In 1596, upon Shakespeare's application, the College of Arms granted his father the now-familiar coat of arms he had taken the first steps to obtain almost twenty years before, and in 1598, John's son – now permitted to call himself "gentleman" – took a 10 percent share in the new Globe playhouse. In 1597, he bought a substantial bourgeois house, called New Place, in Stratford – the garden remains, but Shakespeare's house, several times rebuilt, was torn down in 1759 – and over the next few years Shakespeare spent large sums buying land and making other investments in the town and its environs. Though he worked in London, his family remained in Stratford, and he seems always to have considered Stratford the home he would eventually return to. Something approaching a disinterested appreciation of Shakespeare's popular and professional status appears in Francis Meres's *Palladis Tamia* (1598), a not especially imaginative and perhaps therefore persuasive record of literary reputations. Reviewing contemporary English writers, Meres lists the titles of many of Shakespeare's plays, including one not now known, *Love's Labor's Won,* and praises his "mellifluous & hony-tongued" "sugred Sonnets," which were then circulating in manuscript (they were first collected in 1609). Meres describes Shakespeare as "one of the best" English playwrights of both comedy and tragedy. In *Remains . . . Concerning Britain* (1605), William Camden – a more authoritative source than the imitative Meres – calls Shakespeare one of the "most pregnant witts of these our times" and joins him with such writers as Chapman, Daniel, Jonson, Marston, and Spenser. During the first decades of the seventeenth century, publishers began to attribute numerous play quartos, including some non-Shakespearean ones, to Shakespeare, either by name or initials, and we may assume that they deemed Shakespeare's name and supposed authorship, true or false, commercially attractive.

For the next ten years or so, various records show

Shakespeare's dual career as playwright and man of the theater in London, and as an important local figure in Stratford. In 1608-9 his acting company – designated the "King's Men" soon after King James had succeeded Queen Elizabeth in 1603 – rented, refurbished, and opened a small interior playing space, the Blackfriars theater, in London, and Shakespeare was once again listed as a substantial sharer in the group of proprietors of the playhouse. By May 11, 1612, however, he describes himself as a Stratford resident in a London lawsuit – an indication that he had withdrawn from day-to-day professional activity and returned to the town where he had always had his main financial interests. When Shakespeare bought a substantial residential building in London, the Blackfriars Gatehouse, close to the theater of the same name, on March 10, 1613, he is recorded as William Shakespeare "of Stratford upon Avon in the county of Warwick, gentleman," and he named several London residents as the building's trustees. Still, he continued to participate in theatrical activity: when the new Earl of Rutland needed an allegorical design to bear as a shield, or *impresa*, at the celebration of King James's Accession Day, March 24, 1613, the earl's accountant recorded a payment of 44 shillings to Shakespeare for the device with its motto.

For the last few years of his life, Shakespeare evidently concentrated his activities in the town of his birth. Most of the final records concern business transactions in Stratford, ending with the notation of his death on April 23, 1616, and burial in Holy Trinity Church, Stratford-upon-Avon.

THE QUESTION OF AUTHORSHIP

The history of ascribing Shakespeare's plays (the poems do not come up so often) to someone else began, as it continues, peculiarly. The earliest published claim that someone else wrote Shakespeare's plays appeared in an 1856 article by Delia Bacon in the American journal *Putnam's Monthly* – although an Englishman, Thomas Wilmot, had shared his doubts in private (even secretive) conversations with friends near the end of the eighteenth century. Bacon's was a sad personal history that ended in madness and poverty, but the year after her article, she published, with great difficulty and the bemused assistance of Nathaniel Hawthorne (then United States Consul in Liverpool, England), her *Philosophy of the Plays of Shakspere Unfolded.* This huge, ornately written, confusing farrago is almost unreadable; sometimes its intents, to say nothing of its arguments, disappear entirely beneath near-raving, ecstatic writing. Tumbled in with much supposed "philosophy" appear the claims that Francis Bacon (from whom Delia Bacon eventually claimed descent), Walter Ralegh, and several other contemporaries of Shakespeare's had written the plays. The book had little impact except as a ridiculed curiosity.

Once proposed, however, the issue gained momentum among people whose conviction was the greater in proportion to their ignorance of sixteenth- and seventeenth-century English literature, history, and society. Another American amateur, Catherine P. Ashmead Windle, made the next influential contribution to the cause when she published *Report to the British Museum* (1882), wherein she promised to open "the Cipher of Francis Bacon," though what she mostly offers, in the words of S. Schoenbaum, is "demented allegorizing." An entire new cottage industry grew from Windle's suggestion that the texts contain hidden, cryptographically discoverable ciphers – "clues" – to their authorship; and today there are not only books devoted to the putative ciphers, but also pamphlets, journals, and newsletters.

Although Baconians have led the pack of those seeking a substitute Shakespeare, in *"Shakespeare" Identified* (1920), J. Thomas Looney became the first published

"Oxfordian" when he proposed Edward de Vere, seventeenth earl of Oxford, as the secret author of Shakespeare's plays. Also for Oxford and his "authorship" there are today dedicated societies, articles, journals, and books. Less popular candidates – Queen Elizabeth and Christopher Marlowe among them – have had adherents, but the movement seems to have divided into two main contending factions, Baconian and Oxfordian. (For further details on all the candidates for "Shakespeare," see S. Schoenbaum, *Shakespeare's Lives,* 2nd ed., 1991.)

The Baconians, the Oxfordians, and supporters of other candidates have one trait in common – they are snobs. Every pro-Bacon or pro-Oxford tract sooner or later claims that the historical William Shakespeare of Stratford-upon-Avon could not have written the plays because he could not have had the training, the university education, the experience, and indeed the imagination or background their author supposedly possessed. Only a learned genius like Bacon or an aristocrat like Oxford could have written such fine plays. (As it happens, lucky male children of the middle class had access to better education than most aristocrats in Elizabethan England – and Oxford was not particularly well educated.) Shakespeare received in the Stratford grammar school a formal education that would daunt many college graduates today; and popular rival playwrights such as the very learned Ben Jonson and George Chapman, both of whom also lacked university training, achieved great artistic success, without being taken as Bacon or Oxford.

Besides snobbery, one other quality characterizes the authorship controversy: lack of evidence. A great deal of testimony from Shakespeare's time shows that Shakespeare wrote Shakespeare's plays and that his contemporaries recognized them as distinctive and distinctly superior. (Some of that contemporary evidence is collected in E. K. Chambers, *William Shakespeare: A Study of Facts and Problems,* 2 vols., 1930.) Since that testimony comes from Shakespeare's enemies and theatrical competitors as well as from his co-workers and from the Elizabethan equivalent of literary journalists, it seems unlikely that, if any of these sources had known he was a fraud, they would have failed to record that fact.

Books About Shakespeare's Theater

Useful scholarly studies of theatrical life in Shakespeare's day include: G. E. Bentley, *The Jacobean and Caroline Stage*, 7 vols. (1941-68), and the same author's *The Professions of Dramatist and Player in Shakespeare's Time, 1590-1642* (1986); E. K. Chambers, *The Elizabethan Stage*, 4 vols. (1923); R. A. Foakes, *Illustrations of the English Stage, 1580-1642* (1985); Andrew Gurr, *The Shakespearean Stage*, 3rd ed. (1992), and the same author's *Play-going in Shakespeare's London*, 2nd ed. (1996); Edwin Nungezer, *A Dictionary of Actors* (1929); Carol Chillington Rutter, ed., *Documents of the Rose Playhouse* (1984).

Books About Shakespeare's Life

The following books provide scholarly, documented accounts of Shakespeare's life: G. E. Bentley, *Shakespeare: A Biographical Handbook* (1961); E. K. Chambers, *William Shakespeare: A Study of Facts and Problems*, 2 vols. (1930); S. Schoenbaum, *William Shakespeare: A Compact Documentary Life* (1977); and *Shakespeare's Lives*, 2nd ed. (1991), by the same author. Many scholarly editions of Shakespeare's complete works print brief compilations of essential dates and events. References to Shakespeare's works up to 1700 are collected in C. M. Ingleby et al., *The Shakespeare Allusion-Book*, rev. ed., 2 vols. (1932).

The Texts of Shakespeare

As far as we know, only one manuscript conceivably in Shakespeare's own hand may (and even this is much disputed) exist: a few pages of a play called *Sir Thomas More*, which apparently was never performed. What we do have, as later readers, performers, scholars, students, are printed texts. The earliest of these survive in two forms: quartos and folios. Quartos (from the Latin for "four") are small books, printed on sheets of paper that were then folded in fours, to make eight double-sided pages. When these were bound together, the result was a squarish, eminently portable volume that sold for the relatively small sum of sixpence (translating in modern terms to about $5.00). In folios, on the other hand, the sheets are folded only once, in half, producing large, impressive volumes taller than they are wide. This was the format for important works of philosophy, science, theology, and literature (the major precedent for a folio Shakespeare was Ben Jonson's *Works*, 1616). The decision to print the works of a popular playwright in folio is an indication of how far up on the social scale the theatrical profession had come during Shakespeare's lifetime. The Shakespeare folio was an expensive book, selling for between fifteen and eighteen shillings, depending on the binding (in modern terms, from about $150 to $180). Twenty Shakespeare plays of the thirty-seven that survive first appeared in quarto, seventeen of which appeared during Shakespeare's lifetime; the rest of the plays are found only in folio.

The First Folio was published in 1623, seven years after Shakespeare's death, and was authorized by his fellow actors, the co-owners of the King's Men. This publication was certainly a mark of the company's enormous respect for Shakespeare; but it was also a way of turning the old plays, most of which were no longer current in the playhouse, into ready money (the folio includes only Shakespeare's plays, not his sonnets or other nondramatic verse). Whatever the motives behind the publication of the folio, the texts it preserves constitute the basis for almost all later editions of the playwright's works. The texts, however, differ from those of the earlier quartos, sometimes in minor respects but often significantly – most strikingly in the two texts of *King Lear*, but also in important ways in *Hamlet, Othello,* and *Troilus and Cressida.* (The variants are recorded in the textual notes to each play in the new Pelican series.) The differences in these texts represent, in a sense, the essence of theater: the texts of plays were initially not intended for publication. They were scripts, designed for the actors to perform – the principal life of the play at this period was in performance. And it follows that in Shakespeare's theater the playwright typically had no say either in how his play was performed or in the disposition of his text – he was an employee of the company. The authoritative figures in the theatrical enterprise were the shareholders in the company, who were for the most part the major actors. They decided what plays were to be done; they hired the playwright and often gave him an outline of the play they wanted him to write. Often, too, the play was a collaboration: the company would retain a group of writers, and parcel out the scenes among them. The resulting script was then the property of the company, and the actors would revise it as they saw fit during the course of putting it on stage. The resulting text belonged to the company. The playwright had no rights in it once he had been paid. (This system survives largely intact in the movie industry, and most of the playwrights of Shakespeare's time were as anonymous as most screenwriters are today.) The script could also, of course, continue to change as the tastes of audiences and the requirements of the actors changed. Many – perhaps most – plays were revised when they were reintroduced after any substantial absence from the repertory, or when they were performed

by a company different from the one that originally com-
missioned the play.

Shakespeare was an exceptional figure in this world
because he was not only a shareholder and actor in his
company, but also its leading playwright – he was literally
his own boss. He had, moreover, little interest in the
publication of his plays, and even those that appeared
during his lifetime with the authorization of the company
show no signs of any editorial concern on the part of
the author. Theater was, for Shakespeare, a fluid and
supremely responsive medium – the very opposite of the
great classic canonical text that has embodied his works
since 1623.

The very fluidity of the original texts, however, has
meant that Shakespeare has always had to be edited. Here
is an example of how problematic the editorial project in-
evitably is, a passage from the most famous speech in
Romeo and Juliet, Juliet's balcony soliloquy beginning "O
Romeo, Romeo, wherefore art thou Romeo?" Since the
eighteenth century, the standard modern text has read,

> What's Montague? It is nor hand, nor foot,
> Nor arm, nor face, nor any other part
> Belonging to a man. O be some other name!
> What's in a name? That which we call a rose
> By any other name would smell as sweet.
>
> (II.2.40–44)

Editors have three early texts of this play to work from,
two quarto texts and the folio. Here is how the First
Quarto (1597) reads:

> Whats *Mountague?* It is nor hand nor foote,
> Nor arme, nor face, nor any other part.
> Whats in a name? That which we call a Rose,
> By any other name would smell as sweet:

Here is the Second Quarto (1599):

> Whats *Mountague*? it is nor hand nor foote,
> Nor arme nor face, ô be some other name
> Belonging to a man.
> Whats in a name that which we call a rose,
> By any other word would smell as sweete,

And here is the First Folio (1623):

> What's *Mountague*? it is nor hand nor foote,
> Nor arme, nor face, O be some other name
> Belonging to a man.
> What? in a names that which we call a Rose,
> By any other word would smell as sweete,

There is in fact no early text that reads as our modern text does – and this is the most famous speech in the play. Instead, we have three quite different texts, all of which are clearly some version of the same speech, but none of which seems to us a final or satisfactory version. The transcendently beautiful passage in modern editions is an editorial invention: editors have succeeded in conflating and revising the three versions into something we recognize as great poetry. Is this what Shakespeare "really" wrote? Who can say? What we can say is that Shakespeare always had performance, not a book, in mind.

Books About the Shakespeare Texts

The standard study of the printing history of the First Folio is W. W. Greg, *The Shakespeare First Folio* (1955). J. K. Walton, *The Quarto Copy for the First Folio of Shakespeare* (1971), is a useful survey of the relation of the quartos to the folio. The second edition of Charlton Hinman's *Norton Facsimile* of the First Folio (1996), with a new introduction by Peter Blayney, is indispensable. Stanley Wells, Gary Taylor, John Jowett, and William Montgomery, *William Shakespeare: A Textual Companion*, keyed to the Oxford text, gives a comprehensive survey of the editorial situation for all the plays and poems.

THE GENERAL EDITORS

Introduction

IN 1592 ROBERT GREENE, one of Shakespeare's rivals on the London stage, parodied a line from *3 Henry VI* in a pamphlet called *Greenes Groats-worth of Witte*. Greene turned York's bitter words to Margaret, "O tiger's heart wrapped in a woman's hide!" (I.4.138) into an attack on Shakespeare, whom he accused of having a "tiger's heart wrapped in a player's hide." The parody implies that *3 Henry VI* was a popular play whose memorable lines were well known to Greene's Elizabethan audience. In our own time, however, the Henry VI plays have been over-shadowed by other works, such as *Richard III* or *Henry V*, in which strong protagonists transform English history into dramas of individual psychology. In contrast to some of these more famous Shakespearean histories, the Henry VI plays represent their title character as an uncertainty at the heart of the drama rather than a central figure. Instead of showing how historical circumstances emanate from the monarch's character, these works highlight the inter-dependence of character and circumstance.

Henry VI came to the throne when he was nine months old. The king's personality was thus shaped by public events, perhaps much more than events were ever shaped by the king. This certainly seems to be the as-sumption of Shakespeare's Henry VI plays, which show Henry developing under the influence of politicians try-ing to use him instead of seeking to nurture him. Failure is reciprocal, as conspiracy and rebellion weaken King Henry, and Henry's weakness encourages disorder. In *1 Henry VI* the child-king's aristocratic guardians fight among themselves and neglect both Henry's upbringing and his empire. *2 Henry VI* expands the study of Henry's fall, to embrace all levels of English society. In *3 Henry VI*,

Shakespeare again focuses on the nobles who should be England's leaders, revealing them totally absorbed in the treachery and brutality of civil war.

2 Henry VI saw the start of open hostilities in the Wars of the Roses. After the first battle of Saint Albans, in 1455, the Lancastrians, including King Henry, fled to London. As *3 Henry VI* begins, Richard Duke of York and his followers arrive at the Parliament House in pursuit of the king. York's son Richard, later Richard III, is still carrying the head of his last battle victim, the Duke of Somerset:

> RICHARD *To Somerset's head, which he shows*
> Speak thou for me, and tell them what I did.
> RICHARD DUKE OF YORK
> Richard hath best deserved of all my sons.
> *To the head*
> But is your grace dead, my Lord of Somerset?
> (I.1.16–18)

The picture of the Yorks clowning with Somerset's head recalls the scene in *2 Henry VI* where Jack Cade and his rebels play with the severed heads of two victims, making them kiss (IV.7). Civil war, it appears, brings out barbarity at all social levels. York's son the Earl of Rutland, still a child, is shortly murdered by Clifford, and York himself is captured, humiliated, and stabbed to death by Clifford and Queen Margaret. This parade of horrors brings the play only to the end of Act I.

Like the two earlier plays in the sequence, *3 Henry VI* implicitly compares the orphaned king to several other parent-child pairs. These include York and his sons, Clifford and his dead father, Margaret and the Prince of Wales, and the characters in Act II identified only as "a soldier who has killed his father" and "a soldier who has killed his son." The two Richards, father and son, are alike in ambition and rage. When news comes of York's death, his older son, Edward, cries, "O, speak no more, for I have heard too much" (II.1.48). But Richard feeds on distress: "Say how he died, for I will hear it all" (49). Told that York was taunted by Margaret with a paper crown and a cloth dipped in young Rutland's blood, Richard refuses to mourn: "To weep is to make less the depth of grief; / Tears, then, for babes – blows and revenge for me!" (85-86). Richard reproduces and eventually surpasses York's ferocious appetite for power and revenge.

Henry VI, by contrast, offers only faint echoes of his own legendary father, Henry V. One such reminder occurs when the king arrives at the Parliament House and discovers York sitting in his chair of state:

> Think'st thou that I will leave my kingly throne,
> Wherein my grandsire and my father sat?
> No – first shall war unpeople this my realm.
>
> (I.1.125-27)

Evidently this sensitive and pious king can nevertheless consider slaughtering his people to keep his seat. For a moment, he sounds as ruthless as Clifford, who dedicates himself entirely to revenge and not at all to morality:

> King Henry, be thy title right or wrong,
> Lord Clifford vows to fight in thy defense.
> May that ground gape and swallow me alive
> Where I shall kneel to him that slew my father.
>
> (160-63)

A few lines later, however, York stamps his foot, his soldiers peep out from their hiding places, and Henry agrees without a whimper to make the duke his heir. This abrupt switch from a vow of total war to one of peace makes it clear that Henry's solution to York's aggression derives not from an inability to contemplate armed conflict but from a dread of carrying it out.

Audiences at the Henry VI plays can perhaps sympathize with a king unable to sustain the warlike attitudes of a father he has never seen. By entailing the crown to York and his heirs, however, Henry violates his own responsibilities as a father. To his family, the king can only say, "Pardon me, Margaret; pardon me, sweet son – / The Earl of Warwick and the duke enforced me" (229-30). Margaret and Prince Edward march out to lead the army themselves, and "bashful Henry" withdraws into his mind, where fitful anger fights a losing battle with vivid images of fear:

> Revenged may she be on that hateful duke,
> Whose haughty spirit, wingèd with desire,
> Will coast my crown, and, like an empty eagle,
> Tire on the flesh of me and of my son.
>
> (267-70)

Thereafter, Henry becomes a looker-on rather than a participant in the conflict between Lancaster and York. From the sidelines, he laments the "unnatural" savagery of civil war, which splits households apart. It seems possible to interpret the two soldiers who drag the bodies of their kinfolk on stage as projections of the king's own imagination. A lifetime of experience as a merely symbolic ruler has trained him to focus on emblematic parallels. Thus when the first soldier discovers he has killed his father in battle, and the second discovers he has killed his son, Henry grieves for the "bloody times" that have engulfed them all. Like the two soldiers, however, he regards himself as a victim and not a maker of civil war, dreading censure without admitting fault:

FIRST SOLDIER
> How will my mother for a father's death
> Take on with me, and ne'er be satisfied!

SECOND SOLDIER
> How will my wife for slaughter of my son
> Shed seas of tears, and ne'er be satisfied!

KING HENRY
> How will the country for these woeful chances
> Misthink the king, and not be satisfied!
>
> (II.5.103-8)

Henry attributes events to chance, fortune, and the will of God, never to his own will. On the other side stand the self-reliant Yorks, especially Richard. Even as he struggles to maintain his brother Edward on the throne, Richard, now Duke of Gloucester, also begins a campaign for himself:

> I can add colors to the chameleon,
> Change shapes with Proteus for advantages,
> And set the murderous Machiavel to school.
> Can I do this, and cannot get a crown?
> Tut, were it farther off, I'll pluck it down.
>
> (III.2.191-95)

In the end, Edward is king, but it is Richard and Henry who face off as the champions of two opposing responses to the world: complete resignation to fate and complete defiance. When Richard comes to kill Henry in the Tower, the king's only resistance is prophecy:

> Teeth hadst thou in thy head when thou wast
>   born,
> To signify thou cam'st to bite the world;
> And if the rest be true which I have heard,
> Thou cam'st —
>
> RICHARD DUKE OF GLOUCESTER
> I'll hear no more. Die, prophet, in thy speech,
>   *He stabs him.*
> For this, amongst the rest, was I ordained.
>
> KING HENRY
> Ay, and for much more slaughter after this.
> O, God forgive my sins, and pardon thee.
>   *He dies.*
>
> (V.6.53-60)

Richard admits the truth of Henry's perceptions, but rejects his piety. The heavens may indeed rule Richard's life, but they cannot make him like it:

> Then, since the heavens have shaped my body so,
> Let hell make crooked my mind to answer it.
> I had no father, I am like no father;
> I have no brother, I am like no brother;
> And this word "love," which graybeards call divine,
> Be resident in men like one another
> And not in me – I am myself alone.
>
> (78–84)

The audience knows that Richard does resemble his father and once loved him fiercely, yet now he denies all determining forces except self. Henry refuses to see the world as a place where he can make choices and take action, and Richard refuses to see it any other way. Henry is a good man and Richard is an evil one, but neither is fit to govern, as Shakespeare demonstrates here and in *Richard III*, the last play in the series.

3 Henry VI seems less episodic than the other two Henry VI plays because its major incidents all depict the fluctuating fortunes of the wars between Lancaster and York. Act I shows the aftermath of the first battle of Saint Albans and the death of York at the battle of Wakefield. At the start of Act II, Warwick describes the second battle of Saint Albans, and at the end of the act King Henry observes the battle of Towton (II.5). Henry is taken prisoner in Act III, until Warwick the "kingmaker" changes sides, and takes the crown from Edward (IV.3) and restores it to Henry (IV.6). Act V portrays the battle of Barnet, where Henry was recaptured, and the battle of Tewkesbury, where Margaret was defeated and her son Edward killed. Historically, these events took place over ten years, from 1461 to 1471, and the play is crowded with violent incidents as the balance between the two sides tips back and forth. Yet Shakespeare manages to shape the narrative of these battles into a dramatic structure in which Henry's decline and Margaret's defeat are counterpoised by Edward's rise and the ominous success of Richard.

Although Richard and his brothers mock Clifford for following a woman, "Captain Margaret" (II.6.75), the queen stands in roughly the same relation to Henry as Richard does to his brother Edward. Henry's cause depends on Margaret's military leadership, just as the Yorks' depends on Richard's. The Yorks question Margaret's womanhood –"O tiger's heart wrapped in a woman's hide!" (I.4.138)– and scorn a female general, but these are ritual insults, the equivalent of Margaret's calling Warwick "long-tongued" (II.2.102) or Richard a "foul misshapen stigmatic" (136). Like the other Henry VI plays, this one treats women as little different from men in their motivations and sometimes in their methods. Margaret wants power and revenge, and like the other nobles in the play, she pursues it on the battlefield. The motives of Lady Grey, later Edward IV's Queen Elizabeth, are more obscure. In II.2, she finds herself in the same situation as the young Margaret did at the end of *I Henry VI*, when circumstances propelled her to the throne. Elizabeth, like Margaret, is an ambitious female struggling to advance herself in situations controlled by powerful males. But whether either woman uses her sexuality to angle for marriage with a king or merely watches out for herself is hard to say. Henry's choice of Margaret and Edward's choice of Elizabeth lead their husbands into political trouble, and Elizabeth's response, to seek protection, accords better with conventional notions of how women should behave than Margaret's increasing belligerence. Yet both women evoke pity and fear. Margaret, like the other ruthless warriors in *3 Henry VI*, laughs at the death of her enemy's children and suffers when her child suffers. Both Margaret and Elizabeth fix their hopes on their young sons, both named Prince Edward. At the end of the play, Margaret's Edward is dead and Elizabeth's is still alive. But

Richard of Gloucester lives, too, and the audience has already seen him planning more dynastic butchery.

Because the plays in the Henry VI sequence, including *Richard III*, are closely related and seem to have been written at about the same time, they are known as Shakespeare's first "tetralogy," or four-play series. Although each of these plays is a full-length drama, the later ones continue several of the story lines begun earlier. Their action stretches from the funeral of Henry V in 1422 to the defeat of Richard III in 1485, but they may never have been staged as a continuous series until the twentieth century. Scholars have disagreed about the order in which Shakespeare wrote the plays, some arguing that *1 Henry VI* was drafted after *2 Henry VI* and *3 Henry VI* to provide an introduction. No matter how the Henry VI series was composed or first presented, however, the epilogue to Shakespeare's *Henry V* suggests the playwright's confidence that his audience knew all three plays and thought of them as a sequence:

> Henry the Sixth, in infant bands crowned king
>   Of France and England, did this king succeed;
> Whose state so many had the managing
>   That they lost France, and made his England
>   bleed:
> Which oft our stage hath shown.
>
> (Henry V, Epilogue, 9–13)

Some students of the plays have also wondered whether Shakespeare wrote everything in the first tetralogy, a difficult question in the Tudor-Stuart period, when playwrights routinely collaborated and rewrote one another's work, much as screenwriters do today. Taken as a whole, however, the three Henry VI plays plus *Richard III* present a developing dramatic picture of England's political fortunes during the Wars of the Roses. (The plays of the second tetralogy, *Richard II, 1 Henry IV, 2 Henry IV,* and

Henry V, concern an earlier period, 1399-1420, and are not so closely connected as the first four.)

Although Shakespeare derives the events of *3 Henry VI* largely from the chronicle histories of Edward Hall (1548) and Raphael Holinshed (1587), many of the details are invented. Such mingling of fact and fiction is typical of Shakespeare's method in the English history plays, as he converts his narrative sources into drama. Shakespeare was one of the most important Elizabethan authors of such plays. Some scholars even consider him the first dramatist to use English history to comment on his own era. Yet his works violate most modern ideas of how history should be written. These dramas mingle source material, what we might think of as fact, with material created by the author, or fiction. It seems clear, however, that Elizabethan scholars, writers, and audiences did not look at history the way we do. The chroniclers Hall and Holinshed, for example, gathered their narratives of medieval English history not from primary documents or eyewitness accounts, but from earlier chronicles and literary stories. For the Tudors, the purpose of retelling the history of the period from Richard II to Richard III was not so much to achieve a scientific re-creation of events as to point out morals and cautionary tales. The example of a king such as Henry VI, later perceived as a failure, could help the Elizabethans avoid calamities like the Wars of the Roses. Whether the motives and actions attributed to Henry and his nobles were matters of fact or merely possible explanations seems to have mattered less than the need to avoid behaviors that might lead to similar disasters. Perhaps Henry V was in reality not the consummate warrior-politician that Shakespeare sketches at the start of the first tetralogy, and perhaps society did not really fail Henry VI in the ways shown in these plays. Nevertheless, an Elizabethan might have replied, it could have happened this way, and our era needs to understand and avoid such situations. As William Baldwin put it in

A Mirror for Magistrates (1559), "where the ambitious seek no office, there no doubt offices are duly minist'red; and where offices are duly minist'red, it cannot be chosen but the people are good, whereof must needs follow a good commonweal. For if the officers be good, the people cannot be ill. Thus the goodness or badness of any realm lieth in the goodness or badness of the rulers."

By most measures, the language of the Henry VI plays is stately and formal. The editors of the Oxford Shakespeare have devised what they call a "colloquialism-in-verse" index, charting contractions and other abbreviated linguistic forms, and find these plays to be among the least colloquial Shakespearean dramas. While much sixteenth-century language sounds ornate to the modern ear, comparison of the Henry VI plays to the body of Shakespeare's work shows that the dialogue of this series observes the conventions of formal oratory more than many of his other dramas. The characters speak in balanced, largely end-stopped lines, as when Henry stands and muses on the combatants before him:

> This battle fares like to the morning's war,
>> When dying clouds contend with growing light,
> What time the shepherd, blowing of his nails,
>> Can neither call it perfect day nor night.
> Now sways it this way like a mighty sea
>> Forced by the tide to combat with the wind,
> Now sways it that way like the selfsame sea
>> Forced to retire by fury of the wind.
>
>> (II.5.1-8)

In elaborate rhetorical similes, Henry compares the civil war to the struggle of night with day and the contention of sea and wind. Pauses in thought occur at the ends of lines, which also use rhyme and repetition to enhance the impression that the king is creating an artifact in his mind, setting up an orderly construct to oppose the chaos of battle. His own image of "the shepherd, blowing of his nails" then leads Henry to envision himself as a "homely swain," happily filling up his days with pastoral duties:

> So many hours must I tend my flock,
> So many hours must I take my rest,
> So many hours must I contemplate,
> So many hours must I sport myself,
> So many days my ewes have been with young,
> So many weeks ere the poor fools will ean,
> So many years ere I shall shear the fleece.
> So minutes, hours, days, weeks, months, and years,
> Passed over to the end they were created,
> Would bring white hairs unto a quiet grave.
>
> (31–40)

If being king had been like this – predictable and peaceful – Henry might have served with joy. The echoing figures of formal rhetoric, particularly *anaphora,* or repeated words at the beginnings of clauses, help create a sound picture of the soothing routine that Henry longs for.

Of course, Henry's kingship has not resembled his pastoral daydream, nor, the play implies, could a king ever be merely the shepherd of his people. Authority rests on military power, and a medieval king's power resides in the strength and loyalty of his barons. Henry's warrior father, Henry V, turned power outward to create an empire in France. In the leadership void of his son's regime, however, power turned inward and devoured civil peace. Shakespeare uses the unfortunate reign of Henry VI, whose failure was the fault of many, to explore the dangers of a weak monarchy. He also examines, in his portraits of the Yorks, the kind of mad ambition that leads to tyranny. A monarchical nation must somehow avoid both types, but the only hope offered in *3 Henry VI* seems, like Henry himself, to rely on fate. Those who know their history know the king is right when he predicts that the young

Earl of Richmond will one day provide England with a more stable monarchy:

> This pretty lad will prove our country's bliss.
> His looks are full of peaceful majesty,
> His head by nature framed to wear a crown,
> His hand to wield a scepter, and himself
> Likely in time to bless a regal throne.
> Make much of him, my lords, for this is he
> Must help you more than you are hurt by me.
>   (IV.7.70-76)

At the end of *Richard III*, Richmond will finally end the Wars of the Roses by killing Richard and assuming the throne as Henry VII.

3 Henry VI takes prophecy seriously, as do most of Shakespeare's plays. But the role of fate in this political drama is anything but simple. Pious Henry expresses orthodox resignation as he watches the battle fought in his name: "To whom God will, there be the victory" (II.5.15). Yet as the play shows, Henry's passivity provokes and intensifies the civil wars. The self-reliance of the Yorks, on the other hand, does not make them immune to fate, as Richard acknowledges:

> The midwife wondered and the women cried,
> "O, Jesus bless us, he is born with teeth!"—
> And so I was, which plainly signified
> That I should snarl and bite and play the dog.
>   (V.6.74-77)

Richard both admits and challenges Henry's prophecies, as he also challenges heaven, stabbing the dead king's body and cursing his soul: "Down, down to hell, and say I sent thee thither" (67). Henry's mere acceptance of divine will leads to inertia, while Richard's defiance leads to savagery.

If the play endorses any attitude toward fate, it may be

that of Somerset, who believes Henry's predictions for Richmond, but does not therefore abandon the young earl to his destiny:

> As Henry's late presaging prophecy
> Did glad my heart with hope of this young
>   Richmond,
> So doth my heart misgive me, in these conflicts,
> What may befall him, to his harm and ours.
> Therefore, Lord Oxford, to prevent the worst,
> Forthwith we'll send him hence to Brittany,
> Till storms be past of civil enmity.
>
> (IV.7.92–98)

Henry knows that God's purposes will be fulfilled, but refuses to serve as their active instrument. Richard thinks that God's purposes will be fulfilled, but refuses to submit. Somerset and Oxford, more prudent than either Lancaster or York, manage to resolve the paradox of fate by walking a middle way. They assume that God's will must be done, but do not presume that they know what it is or how it is to be executed.

JANIS LULL
University of Alaska Fairbanks

The Third Part of Henry the Sixth
GENEALOGICAL CHART

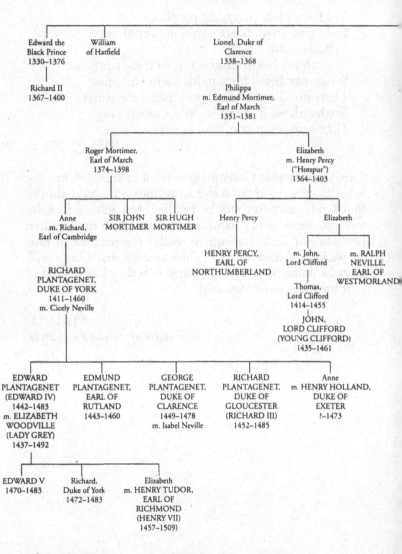

| Edward the Black Prince 1330–1376 | William of Hatfield | Lionel, Duke of Clarence 1338–1368 |

Richard II 1367–1400

Philippa m. Edmund Mortimer, Earl of March 1351–1381

Roger Mortimer, Earl of March 1374–1398

Elizabeth m. Henry Percy ("Hotspur") 1364–1403

Anne m. Richard, Earl of Cambridge

SIR JOHN MORTIMER

SIR HUGH MORTIMER

Henry Percy

Elizabeth

RICHARD PLANTAGENET, DUKE OF YORK 1411–1460 m. Cicely Neville

HENRY PERCY, EARL OF NORTHUMBERLAND

m. John, Lord Clifford

m. RALPH NEVILLE, EARL OF WESTMORLAND

Thomas, Lord Clifford 1414–1455

JOHN, LORD CLIFFORD (YOUNG CLIFFORD) 1435–1461

EDWARD PLANTAGENET (EDWARD IV) 1442–1483 m. ELIZABETH WOODVILLE (LADY GREY) 1437–1492

EDMUND PLANTAGENET, EARL OF RUTLAND 1443–1460

GEORGE PLANTAGENET, DUKE OF CLARENCE 1449–1478 m. Isabel Neville

RICHARD PLANTAGENET, DUKE OF GLOUCESTER (RICHARD III) 1452–1485

Anne m. HENRY HOLLAND, DUKE OF EXETER ?–1473

EDWARD V 1470–1483

Richard, Duke of York 1472–1483

Elizabeth m. HENRY TUDOR, EARL OF RICHMOND (HENRY VII) 1457–1509

❧ Names of characters in the play appear in capitals.
Many persons not significant to *3 Henry VI* are omitted.

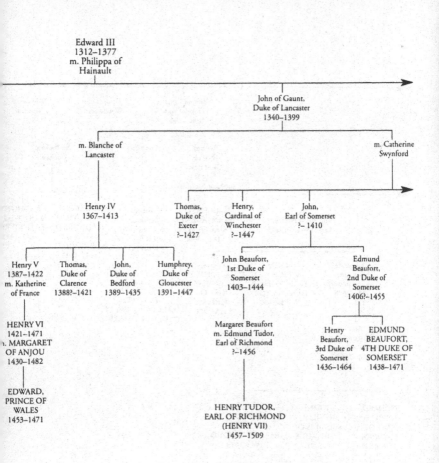

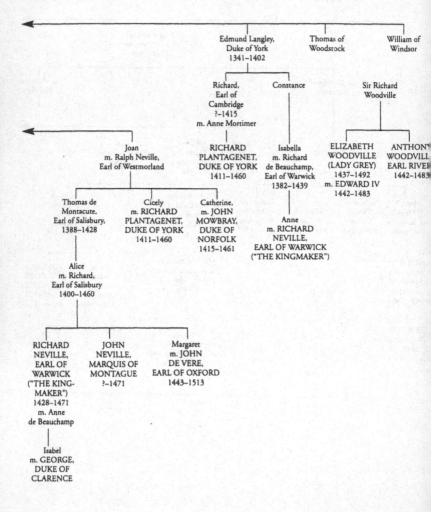

Edmund Langley,
Duke of York
1341–1402

Thomas of
Woodstock

William of
Windsor

Richard,
Earl of
Cambridge
?–1415
m. Anne Mortimer

Constance

Sir Richard
Woodville

Joan
m. Ralph Neville,
Earl of Westmorland

RICHARD
PLANTAGENET,
DUKE OF YORK
1411–1460

Isabella
m. Richard
de Beauchamp,
Earl of Warwick
1382–1439

ELIZABETH
WOODVILLE
(LADY GREY)
1437–1492
m. EDWARD IV
1442–1483

ANTHONY
WOODVILLE
EARL RIVERS
1442–1483

Thomas de
Montacute,
Earl of Salisbury,
1388–1428

Cicely
m. RICHARD
PLANTAGENET,
DUKE OF YORK
1411–1460

Catherine,
m. JOHN
MOWBRAY,
DUKE OF
NORFOLK
1415–1461

Anne
m. RICHARD
NEVILLE,
EARL OF WARWICK
("THE KINGMAKER")

Alice
m. Richard,
Earl of Salisbury
1400–1460

RICHARD
NEVILLE,
EARL OF
WARWICK
("THE KING-
MAKER")
1428–1471
m. Anne
de Beauchamp

JOHN
NEVILLE,
MARQUIS OF
MONTAGUE
?–1471

Margaret
m. JOHN
DE VERE,
EARL OF OXFORD
1443–1513

Isabel
m. GEORGE,
DUKE OF
CLARENCE

Note on the Text

Two versions of this play survive. The first to be published, in octavo format (O, 1595), though undeniably corrupt, appears to derive from a revised, post-performance version of the play later than that included in the First Folio collection (F, 1623), which seems to have been set from a slightly damaged, pre-performance, authorial early draft.

The control text for this new Pelican edition is F, though I do take account of what I believe to be the revisions represented by O where I believe these reflect what happened onstage and where reconstruction seems practically possible.

While this edition uses the traditional folio title for this play, there are powerful arguments for preferring a form of the O title, *The True Tragedy of Richard Duke of York*. The O title is what was used when the text was (piratically) published only a few years after the play's initial performances and so was probably the title by which it was contemporarily known to the playgoing, book-buying public. Moreover, the authority of the F title is undermined because the editor of that volume seems to have regularized the titles of the history plays to conform with his organizational principle, which was that these plays be grouped together, arranged in their historical order, and clearly named after the monarchs whose reigns they cover.

This edition silently regularizes speech prefixes, expands stage directions where this appears necessary, and modernizes all spelling and punctuation. Act divisions are more or less traditional, while scene divisions are made on the basis of a stage cleared of all characters. All substantive departures from the control text apart from these exceptions are recorded below.

The adopted reading is in italics, followed by the F reading in roman.

I.1 19 *hap* hope   69 *EXETER* Westm   78 *mine* my   83 *and that's* that's
105 *Thy* My   120–24 *NORTHUMBERLAND . . . king*– Henry. Peace thou,
and giue King Henry leaue to / speake. Warw. Plantagenet shal speake
first: Heare him Lords, / And be you silent and attentiue too, / For he
that interrupts him, shall not liue.   121 *York* Plantagenet   122 *both*
both both   171 *me* (not in F)   197 *thine* an   200 *nor* neyther   255 *the
utter ruin* vtter ruine   260 *with* (not in F)   262 *from* to   269 *coast* cost
I.2 40 *to Edmund Brook* vnto my   72 *uncles* Vnckle
I.4 51 *buckle* buckler   82 *thy* the   151 *passions move* passions moues
II.1 113 *And . . . thought,* (not in F)   127 *captains* Captiues   131 *an idle*
a lazie   144 *his* the
II.2 92 *our brother out* out me   133 *RICHARD* War.   172 *deniest* denied'st
II.5 38 *weeks* (not in F)   119 *E'en* Men
II.6 6 *commixture* Commixtures   8 *The . . . flies,* (not in F)   42 *EDWARD
DUKE OF YORK* Rich.   43 *RICHARD A* A   44 *EDWARD . . . See* See; *And* Ed.
And   60 *his* is   80 *buy but* buy
III.1 17 *wast* was   24 *adversity* Aduesaries   30 *Is* I: 55 *thou that* thou
96 *in the* the
III.2 3 *lands* Land   28 *whip me then* then whip me   30 *an* if   32 *them*
then   119 *as* your   123 *honorably* honourable
III.3 11 *state* Seat   124 *eternal* externall   156 *Warwick, peace* Warwicke
228 *I'll* I
IV.1 17 *you* (not in F)   28 *my* mine   91 *thy* the   133 *near'st* neere
IV.2 2 *sort* people   12 *come* welcome   15 *towns* Towne
IV.6 4 *stands* stand   8 *Comes* Come
IV.7 11 *prisonment* imprisonment   55 *be confiscate* confiscate
IV.8 71 *MONTGOMERY* Soul.   72 *Ireland*– Ireland, &c.   73 *And* Mount.
And
IV.9 12 *stir* stirre vp
V.1 75 *an* if   78 *an* in   80–83 *GEORGE . . . WARWICK* (not in F)   94 *Jeph-
thah* Iephah   102 *brothers* Brother
V.4 35 *York* (not in F)
V.5 49 *The* (not in F)   76–77 *butcher . . . Richard?* butcher Richard?
V.6 46 *tempests* Tempest   80 *I had . . . like no father;* (not in F)   90–91
Henry . . . the rest, King Henry, and the Prince his Son are gone, /
Clarence thy turne is next, and then the rest
V.7 5 *renowned* Renowne   21 *an* if   25 *and* an earlier state of F reads
"add"; *thou* that   27 *kiss* an earlier state of F reads "'tis"   30 *QUEEN
ELIZABETH* Cla.; *Thanks* Thanke   42 *rests* an earlier state of F reads
"tests"

The Third Part of
Henry the Sixth

Names of the Actors

The House of Lancaster and its supporters:
KING HENRY THE SIXTH, *Duke of Lancaster*
QUEEN MARGARET
PRINCE EDWARD, *their only son*
Edmund Beaufort, DUKE OF SOMERSET
*Henry Tudor, the young Earl of Richmond, his nephew
    (nonspeaking)*
Henry Holland, DUKE OF EXETER, *brother-in-law to
    Edward Duke of York*
Henry Percy, EARL OF NORTHUMBERLAND
John, LORD CLIFFORD, *"Young Clifford" in*
    2 Henry VI
Humphrey, Lord Stafford (nonspeaking)
SOMERVILLE
A LANCASTRIAN SOLDIER *who has killed his father*
A HUNTSMAN *who guards King Edward*

The divided House of Neville:
Richard Neville, EARL OF WARWICK *("Kingmaker"),
    nephew of Richard Duke of York; he initially
    supports York, and later Lancaster*
John Neville, MARQUIS OF MONTAGUE, *Richard's
    brother, a nephew and a supporter of York*
Ralph Neville, EARL OF WESTMORLAND, *first cousin to
    Richard and John, and a supporter of Lancaster*
John de Vere, EARL OF OXFORD, *Richard and John's
    brother-in-law, a supporter of Lancaster*
William, LORD HASTINGS, *Richard and John's
    brother-in-law, a supporter of York*

The House of York and its supporters:

RICHARD PLANTAGENET, DUKE OF YORK

EDWARD PLANTAGENET, *Earl of March, his eldest son, later* DUKE OF YORK, *and later still* KING EDWARD THE FOURTH

ELIZABETH WOODVILLE, LADY GREY, *a widow, later Edward's wife,* QUEEN ELIZABETH

Anthony Woodville, EARL RIVERS, *her brother*

GEORGE PLANTAGENET, *Edward's brother, later* DUKE OF CLARENCE

RICHARD PLANTAGENET, *Edward's brother, later* DUKE OF GLOUCESTER, *and later still King Richard the Third*

EDMUND PLANTAGENET, EARL OF RUTLAND, *Edward's brother*

Rutland's TUTOR, *a chaplain*

SIR JOHN MORTIMER, *Richard Duke of York's uncle*

Sir Hugh Mortimer, Sir John's brother, and so also Richard Duke of York's uncle (nonspeaking)

John Mowbray, DUKE OF NORFOLK

Sir William Stanley (nonspeaking)

William Herbert, Earl of Pembroke (nonspeaking)

SIR JOHN MONTGOMERY

Sir James Harrington, a NOBLEMAN

Two GAMEKEEPERS

Three WATCHMEN

LIEUTENANT OF THE TOWER

The French:

KING LOUIS THE ELEVENTH

LADY BONNE OF SAVOY, *his sister-in-law*

Jean, Lord Bourbon, the French High Admiral, son-in-law to King Louis (nonspeaking)

Others:

A SOLDIER *who has killed his son*
Mayor of Coventry (nonspeaking)
MAYOR OF YORK
ALDERMEN OF YORK
SOLDIERS, MESSENGERS, AND ATTENDANTS

SCENE: *England and France*
*

The Third Part of
Henry the Sixth

∾ **I.1** *A chair of state. Alarum. Enter Richard Planta-*
genet Duke of York, his two sons Edward Earl of
March and Crookback Richard, the Duke of Norfolk,
the Marquis of Montague, and the Earl of Warwick,
with Drummers and Soldiers. They all wear white
roses in their hats.

WARWICK
 I wonder how the king escaped our hands?
RICHARD DUKE OF YORK
 While we pursued the horsemen of the north,
 He slyly stole away and left his men;
 Whereat the great Lord of Northumberland,
 Whose warlike ears could never brook retreat,   5
 Cheered up the drooping army; and himself,
 Lord Clifford, and Lord Stafford, all abreast,
 Charged our main battle's front, and, breaking in,   8
 Were by the swords of common soldiers slain.   9
EDWARD
 Lord Stafford's father, Duke of Buckingham,   *10*
 Is either slain or wounded dangerous.   11
 I cleft his beaver with a downright blow.   12

I.1 The Parliament House, London **s.d.** *Alarum* a trumpet call to arms;
Crookback hunchbacked **5** *brook* endure; *retreat* i.e., the trumpet call signaling retreat **8** *battle's* army's **9** *Were . . . slain* (in *2 Henry VI*, V.2, "Old"
Clifford is killed by York) **11** *dangerous* dangerously **12** *beaver* the face
piece of the helmet; *downright* downward

That this is true, father, behold his blood.
   He shows a bloody sword.
MONTAGUE   *To York*
And, brother, here's the Earl of Wiltshire's blood,
   He shows a bloody sword.
Whom I encountered as the battles joined.
RICHARD   *To Somerset's head, which he shows*
Speak thou for me, and tell them what I did.
RICHARD DUKE OF YORK
Richard hath best deserved of all my sons.
   To the head
But is your grace dead, my Lord of Somerset?

19   Such hap have all the line of John of Ghent.
RICHARD
20   Thus do I hope to shake King Henry's head.
   He holds aloft the head, then throws it down.
WARWICK
And so do I, victorious prince of York.
Before I see thee seated in that throne
Which now the house of Lancaster usurps,
I vow by heaven these eyes shall never close.
25   This is the palace of the fearful king,
And this, *(Pointing to the chair of state)* the regal seat –
   possess it, York,
For this is thine, and not King Henry's heirs'.
RICHARD DUKE OF YORK
Assist me then, sweet Warwick, and I will,
For hither we have broken in by force.
NORFOLK
30   We'll all assist you – he that flies shall die.
RICHARD DUKE OF YORK
31   Thanks, gentle Norfolk. Stay by me, my lords
32   And soldiers – stay, and lodge by me this night.

---

19 *Such . . . Ghent* i.e., may all the descendants of John of Ghent (Gaunt) look for the same fate (Edmund, second Duke of Somerset, was a grandson of John of Ghent, Duke of Lancaster; Henry VI was a great-grandson) 25 *fearful* timid, frightened 31 *gentle* noble 32 s.d. *They go up* (the chair of state, which York occupies, is probably placed on a raised platform)

They go up upon the state.

WARWICK

  And when the king comes, offer him no violence

  Unless he seek to thrust you out perforce.   34

    The Soldiers withdraw.

RICHARD DUKE OF YORK

  The queen this day here holds her Parliament,

  But little thinks we shall be of her council;

  By words or blows here let us win our right.

RICHARD

  Armed as we are, let's stay within this house.

WARWICK

  "The Bloody Parliament" shall this be called,

  Unless Plantagenet, Duke of York, be king,   40

  And bashful Henry deposed, whose cowardice

  Hath made us bywords to our enemies.   42

RICHARD DUKE OF YORK

  Then leave me not, my lords. Be resolute –

  I mean to take possession of my right.

WARWICK

  Neither the king nor he that loves him best –

  The proudest he that holds up Lancaster –   46

  Dares stir a wing if Warwick shake his bells.   47

  I'll plant Plantagenet, root him up who dares.

  Resolve thee, Richard – claim the English crown. 49

    Richard Duke of York sits in the chair. Flourish.

    Enter King Henry, Lord Clifford, the Earls of

    Northumberland and Westmorland, the Duke of

    Exeter, and the rest. They all wear red roses in

    their hats.

KING HENRY

  My lords, look where the sturdy rebel sits –   50

---

34 *perforce* by force 42 *bywords* i.e., objects of scorn 46 *holds up* supports
47 *shake . . . bells* twitches (bells were fastened to the legs of hawks; their
ringing supposedly both increased the falcons' ferocity and further frightened the prey) 49 *Resolve thee* decide firmly; **s.d.** Flourish trumpet fanfare
50 *sturdy* stubborn

51   Even in the chair of state! Belike he means,
        Backed by the power of Warwick, that false peer,
        To aspire unto the crown and reign as king.
        Earl of Northumberland, he slew thy father –
        And thine, Lord Clifford – and you both have vowed
          revenge
        On him, his sons, his favorites, and his friends.

NORTHUMBERLAND
        If I be not, heavens be revenged on me.
58   The hope thereof makes Clifford mourn in steel.

WESTMORLAND
        What, shall we suffer this? Let's pluck him down.
60   My heart for anger burns – I cannot brook it.

KING HENRY
        Be patient, gentle Earl of Westmorland.

CLIFFORD
62   Patience is for poltroons, such as he. *(Indicating York)*
        He durst not sit there had your father lived.
        My gracious lord, here in the Parliament
        Let us assail the family of York.

NORTHUMBERLAND
66   Well hast thou spoken, cousin, be it so.

KING HENRY
67   Ah, know you not the city favors them,
68   And they have troops of soldiers at their beck?

EXETER
        But when the duke is slain, they'll quickly fly.

KING HENRY
70   Far be the thought of this from Henry's heart,
71   To make a shambles of the Parliament House.
        Cousin of Exeter, frowns, words, and threats
        Shall be the war that Henry means to use.
            To York
74   Thou factious Duke of York, descend my throne

---

51 *Belike* it is likely that 58 *steel* armor 62 *poltroons* cowards 66 *cousin* kinsman 67 *the city* i.e., London (as distinct from the court) 68 *beck* command 71 *shambles* slaughterhouse 74 *factious* rebellious

And kneel for grace and mercy at my feet.
I am thy sovereign.

RICHARD DUKE OF YORK   I am thine.

EXETER
For shame, come down – he made thee Duke of York.

RICHARD DUKE OF YORK
It was mine inheritance, as the earldom was.   78

EXETER
Thy father was a traitor to the crown.   79

WARWICK
Exeter, thou art a traitor to the crown   80
In following this usurping Henry.

CLIFFORD
Whom should he follow but his natural king?

WARWICK
True, Clifford, and that's Richard Duke of York.

KING HENRY   *To York*
And shall I stand and thou sit in my throne?

RICHARD DUKE OF YORK
It must and shall be so – content thyself.

WARWICK   *To King Henry*
Be Duke of Lancaster, let him be king.

WESTMORLAND
He is both king and Duke of Lancaster –
And that, the Lord of Westmorland shall maintain.

WARWICK
And Warwick shall disprove it. You forget
That we are those which chased you from the field,   90
And slew your fathers, and, with colors spread,   91
Marched through the city to the palace gates.

NORTHUMBERLAND
Yes, Warwick, I remember it to my grief,
And, by his soul, thou and thy house shall rue it.

---

78 *earldom* i.e., the earldom of March (a title inherited by York from his mother, Anne Mortimer; it was through the Mortimers that he also claimed the crown)   **79** *Thy father . . . crown* (York's father, Richard, Earl of Cambridge, was executed during the reign of Henry V)   **91** *colors* flags

WESTMORLAND   *To York*
  Plantagenet, of thee, and these thy sons,
  Thy kinsmen, and thy friends, I'll have more lives
  Than drops of blood were in my father's veins.
CLIFFORD   *To Warwick*
  Urge it no more, lest that, instead of words,
  I send thee, Warwick, such a messenger
100 As shall revenge his death before I stir.
WARWICK   *To York*
  Poor Clifford, how I scorn his worthless threats.
RICHARD DUKE OF YORK   *To King Henry*
102 Will you we show our title to the crown?
  If not, our swords shall plead it in the field.
KING HENRY
  What title hast thou, traitor, to the crown?
105 Thy father was, as thou art, Duke of York;
  Thy grandfather, Roger Mortimer, Earl of March.
  I am the son of Henry the Fifth,
  Who made the dauphin and the French to stoop
  And seized upon their towns and provinces.
WARWICK
110 Talk not of France, sith thou hast lost it all.
KING HENRY
111 The Lord Protector lost it, and not I.
  When I was crowned, I was but nine months old.
RICHARD
113 You are old enough now, and yet, methinks, you lose.
       To York
  Father, tear the crown from the usurper's head.
EDWARD   *To York*
  Sweet father, do so – set it on your head.
MONTAGUE   *To York*
  Good brother, as thou lov'st and honor'st arms,

---

102 *Will you we* do you wish us to   105 *Thy father . . . York* (York actually inherited his title from his uncle; see ll. 77–79)   110 *sith* since   111 *Lord Protector* i.e., Humphrey, Duke of Gloucester   113 *yet* even now

Let's fight it out and not stand caviling thus.   117
RICHARD
  Sound drums and trumpets, and the king will fly.
RICHARD DUKE OF YORK
  Sons, peace!
NORTHUMBERLAND
  Peace, thou – and give King Henry leave to speak.   120
KING HENRY
  Ah, York, why seekest thou to depose me?
  Are we not both Plantagenets by birth,
  And from two brothers lineally descent?
  Suppose by right and equity thou be king –
  Think'st thou that I will leave my kingly throne,
  Wherein my grandsire and my father sat?
  No – first shall war unpeople this my realm;
  Ay, and their colors, often borne in France,
  And now in England to our heart's great sorrow,
  Shall be my winding-sheet. Why faint you, lords?   130
  My title's good, and better far than his.
WARWICK
  Prove it, Henry, and thou shalt be king.
KING HENRY
  Henry the Fourth by conquest got the crown.
RICHARD DUKE OF YORK
  'Twas by rebellion against his king.   134
KING HENRY   *Aside*
  I know not what to say – my title's weak.
     To York
  Tell me, may not a king adopt an heir?
RICHARD DUKE OF YORK
  What then?
KING HENRY
  An if he may, then am I lawful king –   138
  For Richard, in the view of many lords,
  Resigned the crown to Henry the Fourth,   *140*

---

117 *caviling* quibbling frivolously   120 *leave* permission   130 *winding-sheet* shroud; *faint* lose heart   134 *king* i.e., Richard II   138 *An if* if

Whose heir my father was, and I am his.

RICHARD DUKE OF YORK

142 He rose against him, being his sovereign,
And made him to resign his crown perforce.

WARWICK

Suppose, my lords, he did it unconstrained –
145 Think you 'twere prejudicial to his crown?

EXETER

No, for he could not so resign his crown
147 But that the next heir should succeed and reign.

KING HENRY

Art thou against us, Duke of Exeter?

EXETER

149 His is the right, and therefore pardon me.

RICHARD DUKE OF YORK

150 Why whisper you, my lords, and answer not?

EXETER   *To King Henry*

My conscience tells me he is lawful king.

KING HENRY   *Aside*

All will revolt from me and turn to him.

NORTHUMBERLAND   *To York*

Plantagenet, for all the claim thou lay'st,
Think not that Henry shall be so deposed.

WARWICK

155 Deposed he shall be, in despite of all.

NORTHUMBERLAND

Thou art deceived – 'tis not thy southern power
Of Essex, Norfolk, Suffolk, nor of Kent,
Which makes thee thus presumptuous and proud,
159 Can set the duke up in despite of me.

CLIFFORD

160 King Henry, be thy title right or wrong,
Lord Clifford vows to fight in thy defense.
May that ground gape and swallow me alive

---

142 *him* i.e., Richard II; *being* who was   145 *his crown* his claim to the
crown   147 *But* without ensuring   149 *His* i.e., York's   155 *despite* spite
159 *set the duke up* i.e, as king

Where I shall kneel to him that slew my father.
KING HENRY
O, Clifford, how thy words revive my heart!
RICHARD DUKE OF YORK
Henry of Lancaster, resign thy crown.
What mutter you, or what conspire you, lords?
WARWICK
Do right unto this princely Duke of York,
Or I will fill the house with armèd men
And over the chair of state, where now he sits,
Write up his title with usurping blood.   170
He stamps with his foot, and the Soldiers show
themselves.
KING HENRY
My Lord of Warwick, hear me but one word –
Let me for this my lifetime reign as king.
RICHARD DUKE OF YORK
Confirm the crown to me and to mine heirs,
And thou shalt reign in quiet while thou liv'st.
KING HENRY
I am content. Richard Plantagenet,
Enjoy the kingdom after my decease.
CLIFFORD
What wrong is this unto the prince your son?
WARWICK
What good is this to England and himself?
WESTMORLAND
Base, fearful, and despairing Henry.
CLIFFORD
How hast thou injured both thyself and us?   *180*
WESTMORLAND
I cannot stay to hear these articles.   181
NORTHUMBERLAND
Nor I.

---

170 *usurping blood* i.e., King Henry's **181** *articles* clauses in a legal document (i.e., further details of the agreement)

CLIFFORD
   Come, cousin, let us tell the queen these news.
WESTMORLAND   *To King Henry*
   Farewell, fainthearted and degenerate king,
185   In whose cold blood no spark of honor bides.
                              Exit with his Soldiers.
NORTHUMBERLAND   *To King Henry*
   Be thou a prey unto the house of York,
187   And die in bands for this unmanly deed.
                              Exit with his Soldiers.
CLIFFORD   *To King Henry*
   In dreadful war mayst thou be overcome,
   Or live in peace, abandoned and despised.
                              Exit with his Soldiers.
WARWICK   *To King Henry*
190   Turn this way, Henry, and regard them not.
EXETER   *To King Henry*
   They seek revenge and therefore will not yield.
KING HENRY
   Ah, Exeter.
WARWICK   Why should you sigh, my lord?
KING HENRY
   Not for myself, Lord Warwick, but my son,
   Whom I unnaturally shall disinherit.
195   But be it as it may. *(To York)* I here entail
   The crown to thee and to thine heirs for ever,
   Conditionally, that here thou take thine oath
   To cease this civil war, and whilst I live
   To honor me as thy king and sovereign,
200   And nor by treason nor hostility
   To seek to put me down and reign thyself.
RICHARD DUKE OF YORK
   This oath I willingly take and will perform.
WARWICK
   Long live King Henry. *(To York)* Plantagenet, embrace
      him.

---

185 *bides* resides   **187** *bands* bonds   **195** *entail* bequeath inalienably

Richard Duke of York descends. Henry and York
embrace.

KING HENRY   *To York*
And long live thou, and these thy forward sons.   204

RICHARD DUKE OF YORK
Now York and Lancaster are reconciled.

EXETER
Accursed be he that seeks to make them foes.   206
  Sennet. Here Richard Duke of York's train comes down
  from the state.

RICHARD DUKE OF YORK   *To King Henry*
Farewell, my gracious lord, I'll to my castle.   207
          Exeunt York, Edward, and Richard, with Soldiers.

WARWICK
And I'll keep London with my soldiers.
                                      Exit with Soldiers.

NORFOLK
And I to Norfolk with my followers.
                                      Exit with Soldiers.

MONTAGUE
And I unto the sea from whence I came.   210
                                      Exit with Soldiers.

KING HENRY
And I with grief and sorrow to the court.
  King Henry and Exeter turn to leave.
  Enter Queen Margaret and Prince Edward.

EXETER
Here comes the queen, whose looks bewray her anger.   212
I'll steal away.

KING HENRY   Exeter, so will I.

QUEEN MARGARET
Nay, go not from me – I will follow thee.

KING HENRY
Be patient, gentle queen, and I will stay.

---

204 *forward* spirited   206 s.d. *Sennet* a trumpet call indicating a ceremonial
entrance or exit   207 *castle* i.e, Sandal, near Wakefield, in Yorkshire   212
bewray expose

QUEEN MARGARET
   Who can be patient in such extremes?
   Ah, wretched man, would I had died a maid
   And never seen thee, never borne thee son,
   Seeing thou hast proved so unnatural a father.
220   Hath he deserved to lose his birthright thus?
   Hadst thou but loved him half so well as I,
222   Or felt that pain which I did for him once,
   Or nourished him as I did with my blood,
   Thou wouldst have left thy dearest heartblood there
   Rather than have made that savage duke thine heir
   And disinherited thine only son.

PRINCE EDWARD
   Father, you cannot disinherit me.
   If you be king, why should not I succeed?

KING HENRY
   Pardon me, Margaret; pardon me, sweet son –
230   The Earl of Warwick and the duke enforced me.

QUEEN MARGARET
   Enforced thee? Art thou king, and wilt be forced?
232   I shame to hear thee speak! Ah, timorous wretch,
   Thou hast undone thyself, thy son, and me,
234   And giv'n unto the house of York such head
   As thou shalt reign but by their sufferance.
   To entail him and his heirs unto the crown –
   What is it, but to make thy sepulcher
   And creep into it far before thy time?
   Warwick is Chancellor and the Lord of Calais;
240   Stern Falconbridge commands the narrow seas;
241   The duke is made Protector of the Realm;
   And yet shalt thou be safe? Such safety finds

---

222 *that pain* i.e., the pain of giving birth   232 *shame* am ashamed   234 *giv'n . . . head* i.e., slackened the horse's reins so as to allow him to move his head more freely and, hence, to run more rapidly   240 *Stern . . . seas* (William Neville, Baron Falconbridge and Warwick's uncle, served as Warwick's deputy at Calais in 1459–60, whence he would have commanded the Straits of Dover – the *narrow seas*)   241 *duke* i.e., Richard, Duke of York

The trembling lamb environèd with wolves.   243
Had I been there, which am a seely woman,   244
The soldiers should have tossed me on their pikes   245
Before I would have granted to that act.   246
But thou preferr'st thy life before thine honor.
And seeing thou dost, I here divorce myself
Both from thy table, Henry, and thy bed,
Until that act of Parliament be repealed   250
Whereby my son is disinherited.
The northern lords that have forsworn thy colors
Will follow mine, if once they see them spread –
And spread they shall be, to thy foul disgrace
And the utter ruin of the house of York.
Thus do I leave thee.
       To Prince Edward
                              Come, son, let's away.
Our army is ready – come, we'll after them.

KING HENRY
Stay, gentle Margaret, and hear me speak.

QUEEN MARGARET
Thou hast spoke too much already.
       To Prince Edward
                                 Get thee gone.

KING HENRY
Gentle son Edward, thou wilt stay with me?   260

QUEEN MARGARET
Ay, to be murdered by his enemies.

PRINCE EDWARD   *To King Henry*
When I return with victory from the field,
I'll see your grace. Till then, I'll follow her.

QUEEN MARGARET
Come, son, away – we may not linger thus.
                         Exit with Prince Edward.

---

243 *environèd* surrounded   244 *seely* helpless   245 *pikes* axlike weapons
246 *granted* conceded

KING HENRY
    Poor queen, how love to me and to her son
    Hath made her break out into terms of rage.
    Revenged may she be on that hateful duke,
    Whose haughty spirit, wingèd with desire,
269   Will coast my crown, and, like an empty eagle,
270   Tire on the flesh of me and of my son.
    The loss of those three lords torments my heart.
272   I'll write unto them and entreat them fair.
    Come, cousin, you shall be the messenger.
EXETER
274   And I, I hope, shall reconcile them all.

                              Flourish. Exeunt.

                    *

∾ *I.2 Enter Richard, Edward Earl of March, and the*
    Marquis of Montague.

RICHARD
    Brother, though I be youngest give me leave.
EDWARD
    No, I can better play the orator.
MONTAGUE
    But I have reasons strong and forcible.
    Enter Richard Duke of York.
RICHARD DUKE OF YORK
    Why, how now, sons and brother – at a strife?
    What is your quarrel? How began it first?
EDWARD
    No quarrel, but a slight contention.
RICHARD DUKE OF YORK
    About what?
RICHARD
    About that which concerns your grace and us –

---

269 *coast* approach with hostility, attack, assail; *empty* hungry   **270** *Tire* feed
greedily   **272** *fair* courteously   **274 s.d.** *Flourish* a trumpet fanfare
    I.2 York's castle, Sandal (in Yorkshire)   **1** *give me leave* allow me (to
speak)

The crown of England, father, which is yours.

RICHARD DUKE OF YORK

Mine, boy? Not till King Henry be dead.   *10*

RICHARD

Your right depends not on his life or death.

EDWARD

Now you are heir – therefore enjoy it now.

By giving the house of Lancaster leave to breathe,   *13*

It will outrun you, father, in the end.

RICHARD DUKE OF YORK

I took an oath that he should quietly reign.

EDWARD

But for a kingdom any oath may be broken.

I would break a thousand oaths to reign one year.

RICHARD   *To York*

No – God forbid your grace should be forsworn.

RICHARD DUKE OF YORK

I shall be if I claim by open war.

RICHARD

I'll prove the contrary, if you'll hear me speak.   *20*

RICHARD DUKE OF YORK

Thou canst not, son – it is impossible.

RICHARD

An oath is of no moment being not took   *22*

Before a true and lawful magistrate

That hath authority over him that swears.

Henry had none, but did usurp the place.

Then, seeing 'twas he that made you to depose,   *26*

Your oath, my lord, is vain and frivolous.

Therefore to arms – and, father, do but think

How sweet a thing it is to wear a crown,

Within whose circuit is Elysium   *30*

And all that poets feign of bliss and joy.   *31*

Why do we linger thus? I cannot rest

Until the white rose that I wear be dyed

---

13 *leave to breathe* i.e., a respite   22 *moment* importance   26 *depose* swear
30 *circuit* circumference; *Elysium* classical paradise   31 *feign* imagine

Even in the lukewarm blood of Henry's heart.

RICHARD DUKE OF YORK
Richard, enough! I will be king or die.
To Montague
36 Brother, thou shalt to London presently
And whet on Warwick to this enterprise.
Thou, Richard, shalt to the Duke of Norfolk
39 And tell him privily of our intent.
40 You, Edward, shall to Edmund Brook, Lord Cobham,
41 With whom the Kentishmen will willingly rise.
In them I trust, for they are soldiers
Witty, courteous, liberal, full of spirit.
44 While you are thus employed, what resteth more
But that I seek occasion how to rise,
46 And yet the king not privy to my drift,
Nor any of the house of Lancaster.
Enter a Messenger.
48 But stay, what news? Why com'st thou in such post?

MESSENGER
The queen, with all the northern earls and lords,
50 Intend here to besiege you in your castle.
She is hard by with twenty thousand men,
52 And therefore fortify your hold, my lord.

RICHARD DUKE OF YORK
Ay, with my sword. What – think'st thou that we fear
them?
Edward and Richard, you shall stay with me;
My brother Montague shall post to London.
Let noble Warwick, Cobham, and the rest,
Whom we have left protectors of the king,
58 With powerful policy strengthen themselves,
And trust not simple Henry nor his oaths.

MONTAGUE
60 Brother, I go – I'll win them, fear it not.

---

36 *presently* immediately 39 *privily* secretly 41 *rise* (in rebellion) 44
what resteth more what else remains 46 *privy to* aware of; *drift* intentions
48 *post* haste 52 *hold* stronghold 58 *policy* stratagem

And thus most humbly I do take my leave.   *Exit.*
Enter Sir John Mortimer and his brother Sir Hugh.
RICHARD DUKE OF YORK
Sir John and Sir Hugh Mortimer, mine uncles,
You are come to Sandal in a happy hour.   63
The army of the queen mean to besiege us.
SIR JOHN
She shall not need, we'll meet her in the field.
RICHARD DUKE OF YORK
What, with five thousand men?
RICHARD
Ay, with five hundred, father, for a need.   67
A woman's general – what should we fear?   68
A march sounds afar off.
EDWARD
I hear their drums. Let's set our men in order,
And issue forth and bid them battle straight.   70
RICHARD DUKE OF YORK   *To Sir John and Sir Hugh*
Five men to twenty – though the odds be great,
I doubt not, uncles, of our victory.
Many a battle have I won in France
Whenas the enemy hath been ten to one –   74
Why should I not now have the like success?   *Exeunt.*

                              *

∾ **I.3** *Alarums, and then enter the young Earl of
Rutland and his Tutor, a chaplain.*

RUTLAND
Ah, whither shall I fly to scape their hands?
Enter Lord Clifford with Soldiers.
Ah, tutor, look where bloody Clifford comes.

---

63 *happy* fortunate   67 *for a need* if necessary   68 s.d. *A march* drumbeats
70 *straight* immediately   74 *Whenas* when
   I.3 A battlefield between Sandal and Wakefield s.d. *young Earl* (though
historically the second eldest of York's four sons, Edmund, Earl of Rutland, is
treated in this play as if he were the youngest – only a boy, really – thereby
emphasizing the horror of his murder)   1 *scape* escape

CLIFFORD   *To the Tutor*
Chaplain, away – thy priesthood saves thy life.
As for the brat of this accursèd duke,
Whose father slew my father – he shall die.
TUTOR
And I, my lord, will bear him company.
CLIFFORD
Soldiers, away with him.
TUTOR
Ah, Clifford, murder not this innocent child
9   Lest thou be hated both of God and man.

                                                  Exit, guarded.

   Rutland falls to the ground.
CLIFFORD
10   How now – is he dead already?
Or is it fear that makes him close his eyes?
I'll open them.
RUTLAND   *Reviving*
13   So looks the pent-up lion o'er the wretch
That trembles under his devouring paws,
15   And so he walks, insulting o'er his prey,
And so he comes to rend his limbs asunder.
Ah, gentle Clifford, kill me with thy sword
And not with such a cruel threat'ning look.
Sweet Clifford, hear me speak before I die.
20   I am too mean a subject for thy wrath.
Be thou revenged on men, and let me live.
CLIFFORD
In vain thou speak'st, poor boy. My father's blood
Hath stopped the passage where thy words should
   enter.
RUTLAND
Then let my father's blood open it again.
25   He is a man, and, Clifford, cope with him.

---

9 *of* by   13 *pent-up* caged, hence fierce   15 *insulting* exulting   20 *mean*
lowly   25 *cope* fight

CLIFFORD
    Had I thy brethren here, their lives and thine
    Were not revenge sufficient for me.
    No – if I digged up thy forefathers' graves,
    And hung their rotten coffins up in chains,
    It could not slake mine ire nor ease my heart.   30
    The sight of any of the house of York
    Is as a fury to torment my soul.
    And till I root out their accursèd line,
    And leave not one alive, I live in hell.
    Therefore –
RUTLAND
    O, let me pray before I take my death.
        Kneeling
    To thee I pray: sweet Clifford, pity me.
CLIFFORD
    Such pity as my rapier's point affords.
RUTLAND
    I never did thee harm – why wilt thou slay me?
CLIFFORD
    Thy father hath.   40
RUTLAND   But 'twas ere I was born.
    Thou hast one son – for his sake pity me,
    Lest in revenge thereof, sith God is just,   42
    He be as miserably slain as I.
    Ah, let me live in prison all my days,
    And when I give occasion of offense,
    Then let me die, for now thou hast no cause.
CLIFFORD
    No cause? Thy father slew my father, therefore die.
        He stabs him.
RUTLAND
    Dii faciant laudis summa sit ista tuae.   48
        He dies.

---

30 *slake* lessen   42 *sith* since   48 *Dii . . . tuae* may the gods grant that this
be the height of your fame (Ovid, *Heroides,* 2:66)

CLIFFORD
    Plantagenet – I come, Plantagenet!
50   And this thy son's blood cleaving to my blade
    Shall rust upon my weapon till thy blood,
52   Congealed with this, do make me wipe off both.
                Exit with Rutland's body and Soldiers.

*

❧ **I.4** *Alarum. Enter Richard Duke of York.*

RICHARD DUKE OF YORK
1   The army of the queen hath got the field;
2   My uncles both are slain in rescuing me;
    And all my followers to the eager foe
4   Turn back, and fly like ships before the wind,
    Or lambs pursued by hunger-starvèd wolves.
6   My sons – God knows what hath bechancèd them.
7   But this I know – they have demeaned themselves
    Like men born to renown by life or death.
    Three times did Richard make a lane to me,
10 And thrice cried, "Courage, father, fight it out!"
    And full as oft came Edward to my side,
12 With purple falchion painted to the hilt
    In blood of those that had encountered him.
    And when the hardiest warriors did retire,
    Richard cried, "Charge and give no foot of ground!"
16 [   ]
    And cried, "A crown or else a glorious tomb!
    A scepter or an earthly sepulcher!"

---

52 s.d. *and Soldiers* (It is possible, however, that all attendants left the stage with the tutor at l. 9 s.d. Whether they did or not is important, for upon it depends whether Clifford's murder of young Rutland was witnessed [and so responded, mutely, to] by anyone other than the audience.)
    I.4 The battlefield **1** *got* won **2** *My uncles* Sir John and Sir Hugh Mortimer **4** *Turn back* i.e., turn their backs **6** *bechancèd* happened to **7** *demeaned themselves* i.e., behaved **12** *falchion* curved broadsword **16** *[   ]* (a line is probably missing here, one in which Edward, like his brother Richard, is described as having cried out encouragement to York's forces)

With this, we charged again – but out, alas –
We bodged again, as I have seen a swan   20
With bootless labor swim against the tide   21
And spend her strength with overmatching waves.   22
   A short alarum within.
Ah, hark – the fatal followers do pursue,
And I am faint and cannot fly their fury;
And were I strong, I would not shun their fury.
The sands are numbered that makes up my life.   26
Here must I stay, and here my life must end.
   Enter Queen Margaret, Lord Clifford, the Earl of
   Northumberland, and the young Prince Edward,
   with Soldiers.
Come, bloody Clifford, rough Northumberland –
I dare your quenchless fury to more rage!
I am your butt, and I abide your shot.   30

NORTHUMBERLAND
   Yield to our mercy, proud Plantagenet.

CLIFFORD
   Ay, to such mercy as his ruthless arm,
   With downright payment, showed unto my father.   33
   Now Phaëthon hath tumbled from his car,   34
   And made an evening at the noontide prick.   35

RICHARD DUKE OF YORK
   My ashes, as the phoenix, may bring forth   36
   A bird that will revenge upon you all,   37
   And in that hope I throw mine eyes to heaven,
   Scorning whate'er you can afflict me with.
   Why come you not? What – multitudes, and fear?   40

---

20 *bodged* botched, screwed up   **21** *bootless* fruitless   **22** *with* against; *overmatching* more powerful   **26** *sands* i.e., in the hourglass   **30** *butt* target for archery   **33** *downright payment* i.e., vertical blow (York killed Clifford's father in *2 Henry VI,* V.3.27 s.d.)   **34** *Phaëthon* the son of Apollo, who took his father's sun chariot and, unable to manage it, was dashed to pieces (a conventional symbol of presumption, appropriate here because the sun was a Yorkist device)   **35** *noontide prick* mark on a sundial indicating noon   **36** *phoenix* miraculous bird that died through spontaneous combustion and rose again from its own ashes   **37** *bird* child

CLIFFORD
> So cowards fight when they can fly no further;
> So doves do peck the falcon's piercing talons;
> So desperate thieves, all hopeless of their lives,
> Breathe out invectives 'gainst the officers.

RICHARD DUKE OF YORK
> O, Clifford, but bethink thee once again,
46 And in thy thought o'errun my former time,
> And, if thou canst for blushing, view this face
> And bite thy tongue, that slanders him with cowardice
> Whose frown hath made thee faint and fly ere this.

CLIFFORD
50 I will not bandy with thee word for word,
51 But buckle with thee blows twice two for one.
> *He draws his sword.*

QUEEN MARGARET
> Hold, valiant Clifford: for a thousand causes
> I would prolong a while the traitor's life.
> Wrath makes him deaf – speak thou, Northumberland.

NORTHUMBERLAND
> Hold, Clifford – do not honor him so much
> To prick thy finger though to wound his heart.
57 What valor were it when a cur doth grin
> For one to thrust his hand between his teeth
59 When he might spurn him with his foot away?
60 It is war's prize to take all vantages,
61 And ten to one is no impeach of valor.
> *They fight and take York.*

CLIFFORD
62 Ay, ay, so strives the woodcock with the gin.

NORTHUMBERLAND
63 So doth the cony struggle in the net.

---

46 *o'errun* review   50 *bandy* exchange   51 *buckle* grapple, engage   57 *grin* snarl   59 *spurn* kick   60 *prize* reward; *vantages* opportunities   61 *is no impeach of* does not call into question (our)   62 *woodcock* (proverbially stupid, as was the *cony,* l. 63); *gin* engine, trap   63 *cony* rabbit

RICHARD DUKE OF YORK
  So triumph thieves upon their conquered booty,
  So true men yield, with robbers so o'ermatched.   65
NORTHUMBERLAND   *To the Queen*
  What would your grace have done unto him now?
QUEEN MARGARET
  Brave warriors, Clifford and Northumberland,
  Come make him stand upon this molehill here,   68
  That wrought at mountains with outstretchèd arms   69
  Yet parted but the shadow with his hand.   70
    To York
  What – was it you that would be England's king?
  Was't you that reveled in our Parliament,   72
  And made a preachment of your high descent?   73
  Where are your mess of sons to back you now?   74
  The wanton Edward and the lusty George?
  And where's that valiant crookback prodigy,   76
  Dickie, your boy, that with his grumbling voice
  Was wont to cheer his dad in mutinies?   78
  Or with the rest where is your darling Rutland?
  Look, York, I stained this napkin with the blood   80
  That valiant Clifford with his rapier's point
  Made issue from the bosom of thy boy.
  And if thine eyes can water for his death,
  I give thee this to dry thy cheeks withal.   84
  Alas, poor York, but that I hate thee deadly
  I should lament thy miserable state.
  I prithee, grieve, to make me merry, York.
  What – hath thy fiery heart so parched thine entrails
  That not a tear can fall for Rutland's death?
  Why art thou patient, man? Thou shouldst be mad,   90
  And I, to make thee mad, do mock thee thus.

---

65 *true* honest   68 *stand . . . here* (with allusion to the "king of the molehill,"
a term of contempt)   69 *wrought* reached   70 *but* only   72 *reveled* enjoyed
yourself   73 *preachment* sermon   74 *mess of* group of four   76 *prodigy* mon-
ster   78 *mutinies* rebellions   80 *napkin* handkerchief   84 *withal* with

Stamp, rave, and fret, that I may sing and dance.
93 Thou wouldst be fee'd, I see, to make me sport.
York cannot speak unless he wear a crown.
  To her Men
A crown for York, and, lords, bow low to him.
Hold you his hands whilst I do set it on.
  She puts a paper crown on York's head.
97 Ay, marry, sir, now looks he like a king,
Ay, this is he that took King Henry's chair,
And this is he was his adopted heir.
100 But how is it that great Plantagenet
Is crowned so soon and broke his solemn oath?
As I bethink me, you should not be king
Till our King Henry had shook hands with death.
104 And will you pale your head in Henry's glory,
And rob his temples of the diadem
Now, in his life, against your holy oath?
O, 'tis a fault too, too, unpardonable.
Off with the crown,
  She knocks it from his head.
                    and with the crown his head,
109 And whilst we breathe, take time to do him dead.

CLIFFORD
110 That is my office for my father's sake.

QUEEN MARGARET
111 Nay, stay – let's hear the orisons he makes.

RICHARD DUKE OF YORK
She-wolf of France, but worse than wolves of France,
Whose tongue more poisons than the adder's tooth –
114 How ill-beseeming is it in thy sex
115 To triumph like an Amazonian trull
116 Upon their woes whom fortune captivates!

---

93 *fee'd* paid   **97** *marry* by the Virgin Mary (with weakened force)   **104** *pale* encircle   **109** *breathe* rest; *do him dead* kill him   **111** *orisons* prayers   **114** *ill-beseeming* inappropriate, unbecoming   **115** *Amazonian* (the Amazons, who figure in classical myth, were a legendary race of female warriors); *trull* whore   **116** *captivates* subdues

But that thy face is visorlike, unchanging,   117
Made impudent with use of evil deeds,
I would essay, proud queen, to make thee blush.   119
To tell thee whence thou cam'st, of whom derived,   120
Were shame enough to shame thee – wert thou not
  shameless.
Thy father bears the type of King of Naples,   122
Of both the Sicils, and Jerusalem –   123
Yet not so wealthy as an English yeoman.   124
Hath that poor monarch taught thee to insult?
It needs not, nor it boots thee not, proud queen,   126
Unless the adage must be verified   127
That beggars mounted run their horse to death.
'Tis beauty that doth oft make women proud –
But, God he knows, thy share thereof is small;   130
'Tis virtue that doth make them most admired –
The contrary doth make thee wondered at;
'Tis government that makes them seem divine –   133
The want thereof makes thee abominable.
Thou art as opposite to every good
As the antipodes are unto us,   136
Or as the south to the septentrion.   137
O tiger's heart wrapped in a woman's hide!
How couldst thou drain the lifeblood of the child
To bid the father wipe his eyes withal,   140
And yet be seen to bear a woman's face?
Women are soft, mild, pitiful, and flexible –   142
Thou stern, obdurate, flinty, rough, remorseless.
Bidd'st thou me rage? Why, now thou hast thy wish.
Wouldst have me weep? Why, now thou hast thy will.

---

117 *But that* were it not that; *visorlike* expressionless, masklike (prostitutes
sometimes wore masks)   119 *essay* try   122 *type* title   123 *both the Sicils*
i.e., Sicily and Naples   124 *yeoman* landowner (below the rank of gentleman)   126 *boots* profits   127 *adage* proverb   133 *government* self-control
136 *antipodes* (1) the other side of the world, (2) those who live there   137
septentrion seven stars of the constellation of the Great Bear (i.e., north)
142 *pitiful* compassionate

For raging wind blows up incessant showers,

147   And when the rage allays the rain begins.

148   These tears are my sweet Rutland's obsequies,
And every drop cries vengeance for his death

150   'Gainst thee, fell Clifford, and thee, false French-
woman.

NORTHUMBERLAND

151   Beshrew me, but his passions move me so
That hardly can I check my eyes from tears.

RICHARD DUKE OF YORK

That face of his the hungry cannibals
Would not have touched, would not have stained with
blood –
But you are more inhuman, more inexorable,

156   O, ten times more than tigers of Hyrcania.

157   See, ruthless queen, a hapless father's tears.
This cloth thou dipped'st in blood of my sweet boy,
And I with tears do wash the blood away.

160   Keep thou the napkin and go boast of this,

161   And if thou tell'st the heavy story right,
Upon my soul the hearers will shed tears,
Yea, even my foes will shed fast-falling tears
And say, "Alas, it was a piteous deed."
There, take the crown – and with the crown, my curse:
And in thy need such comfort come to thee
As now I reap at thy too cruel hand.
Hardhearted Clifford, take me from the world.
My soul to heaven, my blood upon your heads.

NORTHUMBERLAND

170   Had he been slaughterman to all my kin,
I should not, for my life, but weep with him,

172   To see how inly sorrow gripes his soul.

---

147 *allays* diminishes   148 *obsequies* funeral rites   150 *fell* cruel   151
Beshrew curse   156 *Hyrcania* a region of ancient Persia (the reference to the
fierceness of Hyrcanian tigers derives ultimately from the *Aeneid*, 4:366–67)
157 *hapless* luckless   161 *heavy* sorrowful   172 *inly* heartfelt; *gripes* grieves,
afflicts, distresses

QUEEN MARGARET
   What – weeping-ripe, my Lord Northumberland?   173
   Think but upon the wrong he did us all,
   And that will quickly dry thy melting tears.   175

CLIFFORD
   Here's for my oath, here's for my father's death.
     He stabs York.

QUEEN MARGARET
   And here's to right our gentle-hearted king.
     She stabs York.

RICHARD DUKE OF YORK
   Open thy gate of mercy, gracious God –
   My soul flies through these wounds to seek out thee.
     He dies.

QUEEN MARGARET
   Off with his head and set it on York gates,   *180*
   So York may overlook the town of York.
     Flourish. Exeunt with York's body.

          *

❧ **II.1** *A march. Enter Edward Earl of March and*
    Richard, with a Drummer and Soldiers.

EDWARD
   I wonder how our princely father scaped,
   Or whether he be scaped away or no
   From Clifford's and Northumberland's pursuit.
   Had he been ta'en we should have heard the news;
   Had he been slain we should have heard the news;
   Or had he scaped, methinks we should have heard
   The happy tidings of his good escape.
   How fares my brother? Why is he so sad?

---

173 *weeping-ripe* ready for weeping   175 *melting tears* tears arising from a softened heart
  II.1 Fields in the Marches (the border between Wales and England)

RICHARD

I cannot joy until I be resolved
10 Where our right valiant father is become.
I saw him in the battle range about,
12 And watched him how he singled Clifford forth.
Methought he bore him in the thickest troop,
14 As doth a lion in a herd of neat;
Or as a bear encompassed round with dogs,
16 Who having pinched a few and made them cry,
The rest stand all aloof and bark at him.
So fared our father with his enemies;
So fled his enemies my warlike father.
20 Methinks 'tis prize enough to be his son.
      Three suns appear in the air.
See how the morning opes her golden gates
And takes her farewell of the glorious sun.
How well resembles it the prime of youth,
24 Trimmed like a younker prancing to his love!

EDWARD

25 Dazzle mine eyes, or do I see three suns?

RICHARD

Three glorious suns, each one a perfect sun;
27 Not separated with the racking clouds,
But severed in a pale clear-shining sky.
      The three suns begin to join.
See, see – they join, embrace, and seem to kiss,
30 As if they vowed some league inviolable.
Now are they but one lamp, one light, one sun.
32 In this the heaven figures some event.

EDWARD

'Tis wondrous strange, the like yet never heard of.
34 I think it cites us, brother, to the field,

---

10 *Where . . . is become* what has happened to . . . 12 *forth* out 14 *neat*
cattle 16 *pinched* bitten 20 *prize* privilege 24 *Trimmed* dressed up;
younker young man 25 *Dazzle mine eyes* do my eyes blur 27 *racking* passing 32 *figures* foretells 34 *cites* urges

That we, the sons of brave Plantagenet,
Each one already blazing by our meeds,   36
Should notwithstanding join our lights together
And overshine the earth as this the world.   38
Whate'er it bodes, henceforward will I bear
Upon my target three fair-shining suns.   40

RICHARD
Nay, bear three daughters – by your leave I speak it –   41
You love the breeder better than the male.   42
   Enter one blowing a horn.
But what art thou whose heavy looks foretell
Some dreadful story hanging on thy tongue?

MESSENGER
Ah, one that was a woeful looker-on
Whenas the noble Duke of York was slain –   46
Your princely father and my loving lord.

EDWARD
O, speak no more, for I have heard too much.

RICHARD
Say how he died, for I will hear it all.

MESSENGER
Environèd he was with many foes,   50
And stood against them as the hope of Troy   51
Against the Greeks that would have entered Troy.
But Hercules himself must yield to odds;
And many strokes, though with a little ax,
Hews down and fells the hardest-timbered oak.
By many hands your father was subdued,
But only slaughtered by the ireful arm
Of unrelenting Clifford and the queen,
Who crowned the gracious duke in high despite,   59
Laughed in his face, and when with grief he wept,   60

---

36 *meeds* merits   38 *this* i.e., this phenomenon   40 *target* shield   41
daughters (with obvious pun on *suns*, l. 40)   42 *breeder* female; **s.d.** *blowing
a horn* (indicating that the messenger is a post rider)   46 *Whenas* when   50
Environèd surrounded   51 *hope of Troy* i.e., Hector   59 *in high despite* with
great contempt

The ruthless queen gave him to dry his cheeks
A napkin steepèd in the harmless blood
Of sweet young Rutland, by rough Clifford slain;
And after many scorns, many foul taunts,
They took his head, and on the gates of York
They set the same; and there it doth remain,
The saddest spectacle that e'er I viewed.

EDWARD
Sweet Duke of York, our prop to lean upon,
69   Now thou art gone, we have no staff, no stay.
70   O Clifford, boist'rous Clifford – thou hast slain
The flower of Europe for his chivalry,
And treacherously hast thou vanquished him –
For hand to hand he would have vanquished thee.
74   Now my soul's palace is become a prison.
75   Ah, would she break from hence that this my body
Might in the ground be closèd up in rest.
For never henceforth shall I joy again –
Never, O never, shall I see more joy.

RICHARD
I cannot weep, for all my body's moisture
80   Scarce serves to quench my furnace-burning heart;
Nor can my tongue unload my heart's great burden,
82   For selfsame wind that I should speak withal
Is kindling coals that fires all my breast,
And burns me up with flames that tears would quench.
To weep is to make less the depth of grief;
Tears, then, for babes – blows and revenge for me!
87   Richard, I bear thy name; I'll venge thy death
Or die renownèd by attempting it.

EDWARD
His name that valiant duke hath left with thee,
90   His dukedom and his chair with me is left.

RICHARD
91   Nay, if thou be that princely eagle's bird,

---

69 *stay* support 70 *boist'rous* savage 74 *my soul's palace* i.e, my body 75
she i.e., my soul 82 *wind* breath 87 *venge* revenge 91 *bird* young

Show thy descent by gazing 'gainst the sun: 92
For "chair and dukedom," "throne and kingdom" say –   93
Either that is thine or else thou wert not his.
> *March. Enter the Earl of Warwick and the Marquis of*
> *Montague, with Drummers, an Ensign, and Soldiers.*

WARWICK
How now, fair lords? What fare? What news abroad?   95
RICHARD
Great Lord of Warwick, if we should recount
Our baleful news, and at each word's deliverance   97
Stab poniards in our flesh till all were told,   98
The words would add more anguish than the wounds.
O valiant lord, the Duke of York is slain.   *100*
EDWARD
O Warwick, Warwick! That Plantagenet,
Which held thee dearly as his soul's redemption,
Is by the stern Lord Clifford done to death.
WARWICK
Ten days ago I drowned these news in tears.
And now, to add more measure to your woes,
I come to tell you things sith then befall'n.   106
After the bloody fray at Wakefield fought,
Where your brave father breathed his latest gasp,   108
Tidings, as swiftly as the posts could run,   109
Were brought me of your loss and his depart.   110
I then in London, keeper of the king,
Mustered my soldiers, gathered flocks of friends,
And, very well appointed as I thought,   113
Marched toward Saint Albans to intercept the queen,
Bearing the king in my behalf along –
For by my scouts I was advertisèd   116

---

92 *gazing 'gainst the sun* (Eagles, according to Pliny and many later writers, could gaze at the sun without blinking. The *sun* here symbolizes the king; the *eagle* is an allusion to a Yorkist badge.)   93 *chair* (symbol of a duke's author-ity, as *throne* is of a king's)   95 *What fare?* How goes it?   97 *baleful* deadly   98 *poniards* daggers   106 *sith* since   108 *latest* last   109 *posts* messengers   110 *depart* death   113 *appointed* equipped   116 *advertisèd* informed

That she was coming with a full intent
118 To dash our late decree in Parliament
Touching King Henry's oath and your succession.
120 Short tale to make, we at Saint Albans met,
121 Our battles joined, and both sides fiercely fought;
But whether 'twas the coldness of the king,
Who looked full gently on his warlike queen,
124 That robbed my soldiers of their heated spleen,
Or whether 'twas report of her success,
Or more than common fear of Clifford's rigor –
Who thunders to his captains, "Blood and death!" –
I cannot judge; but, to conclude with truth,
Their weapons like to lightning came and went;
130 Our soldiers', like the night owl's lazy flight,
131 Or like an idle thresher with a flail,
Fell gently down, as if they struck their friends.
I cheered them up with justice of our cause,
With promise of high pay, and great rewards.
But all in vain. They had no heart to fight,
And we in them no hope to win the day.
So that we fled – the king unto the queen,
Lord George your brother, Norfolk, and myself
139 In haste, posthaste, are come to join with you.
140 For in the Marches here we heard you were,
141 Making another head to fight again.

EDWARD
Where is the Duke of Norfolk, gentle Warwick?
And when came George from Burgundy to England?

WARWICK
Some six miles off the duke is with his soldiers;
And for your brother – he was lately sent

---

118 *late* recent   121 *battles* armies   124 *heated spleen* i.e., warlike mood
131 *a flail* an instrument for threshing (a stout stick joined to a longer handle by a leather thong)   139 *posthaste* as speedily as postriders   140 *Marches*
Welsh borders   141 *Making . . . head* gathering . . . force

From your kind aunt, Duchess of Burgundy,   146
With aid of soldiers to this needful war.

RICHARD
'Twas odd belike when valiant Warwick fled.   148
Oft have I heard his praises in pursuit,   149
But ne'er till now his scandal of retire.   150

WARWICK
Nor now my scandal, Richard, dost thou hear –
For thou shalt know this strong right hand of mine
Can pluck the diadem from faint Henry's head   153
And wring the aweful scepter from his fist,   154
Were he as famous and as bold in war
As he is famed for mildness, peace, and prayer.

RICHARD
I know it well, Lord Warwick – blame me not.
'Tis love I bear thy glories make me speak.
But in this troublous time what's to be done?
Shall we go throw away our coats of steel,   160
And wrap our bodies in black mourning gowns,
Numb'ring our Ave Maries with our beads?   162
Or shall we on the helmets of our foes
Tell our devotion with revengeful arms?   164
If for the last, say "ay," and to it, lords.

WARWICK
Why, therefore Warwick came to seek you out,
And therefore comes my brother Montague.
Attend me, lords. The proud insulting queen,
With Clifford and the haught Northumberland,   169
And of their feather many more proud birds,   170

---

146 *aunt . . . Burgundy* (Isabel, Duchess of Burgundy, was a granddaughter
of John of Ghent and a distant cousin to Edward. Holinshed says that
George and Richard were sent for protection to the Duke of Burgundy after
York's death and remained with him until Edward was crowned.)   148
'Twas odd belike no doubt the odds were heavily against him   149 *pursuit*
i.e., of enemies   150 *scandal of retire* disgrace because of retreating   153
faint weak   154 *aweful* awe-inspiring   162 *Ave Maries* Hail Marys (prayers
to the Virgin Mary)   164 *Tell our devotion* (1) count off our prayers, as on a
rosary, (2) declare our love (ironically)   169 *haught* haughty

171 Have wrought the easy-melting king like wax.
       To Edward
     He swore consent to your succession,
173 His oath enrollèd in the Parliament.
     And now to London all the crew are gone,
     To frustrate both his oath and what beside
176 May make against the house of Lancaster.
     Their power, I think, is thirty thousand strong.
     Now, if the help of Norfolk and myself,
179 With all the friends that thou, brave Earl of March,
180 Amongst the loving Welshmen canst procure,
     Will but amount to five and twenty thousand,
182 Why, *via*, to London will we march,
     And once again bestride our foaming steeds,
     And once again cry "Charge!" upon our foes –
     But never once again turn back and fly.
RICHARD
     Ay, now methinks I hear great Warwick speak.
187 Ne'er may he live to see a sunshine day
     That cries "Retire!" if Warwick bid him stay.
EDWARD
     Lord Warwick, on thy shoulder will I lean,
190 And when thou fail'st – as God forbid the hour –
191 Must Edward fall, which peril heaven forfend!
WARWICK
     No longer Earl of March, but Duke of York;
193 The next degree is England's royal throne –
     For King of England shalt thou be proclaimed
     In every borough as we pass along,
     And he that throws not up his cap for joy,
     Shall for the fault make forfeit of his head.
     King Edward, valiant Richard, Montague –
     Stay we no longer dreaming of renown,

---

171 *wrought* persuaded; *easy-melting* softhearted, easily swayed   173 *enrollèd* officially recorded   176 *make* tell   179 *Earl of March* i.e., Edward (his title before York's death; see l. 192)   182 *via* onward   187 *he* i.e., anyone   191 *forfend* forbid   193 *degree* rank

But sound the trumpets and about our task.   200

RICHARD
   Then, Clifford, were thy heart as hard as steel,
   As thou hast shown it flinty by thy deeds,
   I come to pierce it or to give thee mine.

EDWARD DUKE OF YORK
   Then strike up drums – God and Saint George for us!   204
      Enter a Messenger.

WARWICK
   How now? What news?

MESSENGER
   The Duke of Norfolk sends you word by me
   The queen is coming with a puissant host,   207
   And craves your company for speedy counsel.

WARWICK
   Why then it sorts. Brave warriors, let's away.   209
                                    March. Exeunt.

                            *

∾ **II.2** *Richard Duke of York's head is thrust out, above.*
   Flourish. Enter King Henry, Queen Margaret, Lord
   Clifford, the Earl of Northumberland, and young
   Prince Edward, with a Drummer and Trumpeters.

QUEEN MARGARET
   Welcome, my lord, to this brave town of York.
   Yonder's the head of that arch-enemy
   That sought to be encompassed with your crown.
   Doth not the object cheer your heart, my lord?

KING HENRY
   Ay, as the rocks cheer them that fear their wreck.   5
   To see this sight, it irks my very soul.
   Withhold revenge, dear God – 'tis not my fault,
   Nor wittingly have I infringed my vow.   8

---

204 *Saint George* the patron saint of England · 207 *puissant* powerful   209
sorts works out well
- II.2 Before the walls of York   5 *wreck* ruin   8 *wittingly* knowingly

CLIFFORD

9 My gracious liege, this too much lenity
10 And harmful pity must be laid aside.
To whom do lions cast their gentle looks?
Not to the beast that would usurp their den.
Whose hand is that the forest bear doth lick?
14 Not his that spoils her young before her face.
Who scapes the lurking serpent's mortal sting?
Not he that sets his foot upon her back.
The smallest worm will turn, being trodden on,
And doves will peck in safeguard of their brood.
19 Ambitious York did level at thy crown,
20 Thou smiling while he knit his angry brows.
He, but a duke, would have his son a king,
22 And raise his issue like a loving sire;
Thou, being a king, blest with a goodly son,
Didst yield consent to disinherit him,
Which argued thee a most unloving father.
26 Unreasonable creatures feed their young,
And though man's face be fearful to their eyes,
Yet, in protection of their tender ones,
Who hath not seen them, even with those wings
30 Which sometime they have used with fearful flight,
Make war with him that climbed unto their nest,
Offering their own lives in their young's defense?
For shame, my liege, make them your precedent!
Were it not pity that this goodly boy
Should lose his birthright by his father's fault,
And long hereafter say unto his child
"What my great-grandfather and grandsire got
38 My careless father fondly gave away"?
Ah, what a shame were this! Look on the boy,
40 And let his manly face, which promiseth

---

9 *liege* sovereign; *lenity* gentleness   14 *spoils* destroys   19 *level* aim   22 *raise* promote; *issue* offspring   26 *Unreasonable* not endowed with reason   38 *fondly* foolishly

Successful fortune, steel thy melting heart
To hold thine own and leave thine own with him.

KING HENRY
Full well hath Clifford played the orator,
Inferring arguments of mighty force.   44
But, Clifford, tell me – didst thou never hear
That things ill got had ever bad success?   46
And happy always was it for that son   47
Whose father for his hoarding went to hell?   48
I'll leave my son my virtuous deeds behind,
And would my father had left me no more.   50
For all the rest is held at such a rate   51
As brings a thousandfold more care to keep
Than in possession any jot of pleasure.
Ah, cousin York, would thy best friends did know
How it doth grieve me that thy head is here.

QUEEN MARGARET
My lord, cheer up your spirits – our foes are nigh,
And this soft courage makes your followers faint.   57
You promised knighthood to our forward son.   58
Unsheathe your sword and dub him presently.   59
Edward, kneel down.   60
    Prince Edward kneels.

KING HENRY
Edward Plantagenet, arise a knight –
And learn this lesson: draw thy sword in right.

PRINCE EDWARD *Rising*
My gracious father, by your kingly leave,
I'll draw it as apparent to the crown,   64
And in that quarrel use it to the death.   65

CLIFFORD
Why, that is spoken like a toward prince.   66

---

44 *Inferring* adducing 46 *success* outcome 47 *happy . . . it* were things always good 48 *for* because of 51 *rate* cost 57 *faint* fainthearted 58 *forward* high-spirited 59 *dub him* make him a knight; *presently* immediately 64 *apparent* heir 65 *quarrel* cause 66 *toward* bold

Enter a Messenger.

MESSENGER
Royal commanders, be in readiness –
For with a band of thirty thousand men
69 Comes Warwick backing of the Duke of York;
70 And in the towns, as they do march along,
Proclaims him king, and many fly to him.
72 Deraign your battle, for they are at hand.

CLIFFORD   *To King Henry*
I would your highness would depart the field –
The queen hath best success when you are absent.

QUEEN MARGARET   *To King Henry*
Ay, good my lord, and leave us to our fortune.

KING HENRY
Why, that's my fortune too – therefore I'll stay.

NORTHUMBERLAND
Be it with resolution then to fight.

PRINCE EDWARD   *To King Henry*
My royal father, cheer these noble lords
And hearten those that fight in your defense.
80 Unsheathe your sword, good father; cry "Saint
George!"

March. Enter Edward Duke of York, the Earl of
Warwick, Richard, George, the Duke of Norfolk,
the Marquis of Montague, and Soldiers.

EDWARD DUKE OF YORK
Now, perjured Henry, wilt thou kneel for grace,
And set thy diadem upon my head –
83 Or bide the mortal fortune of the field?

QUEEN MARGARET
84 Go rate thy minions, proud insulting boy!
Becomes it thee to be thus bold in terms
Before thy sovereign and thy lawful king?

---

69 *backing of* in support of; *Duke of York* i.e., Edward   **72** *Deraign your battle* deploy your forces   **83** *bide* await; *mortal* fatal   **84** *rate thy minions* chide your favorites

EDWARD DUKE OF YORK
  I am his king, and he should bow his knee.
  I was adopted heir by his consent.
GEORGE   *To Queen Margaret*
  Since when his oath is broke – for, as I hear,
  You that are king, though he do wear the crown,   90
  Have caused him by new act of Parliament
  To blot our brother out, and put his own son in.
CLIFFORD
  And reason too –
  Who should succeed the father but the son?
RICHARD
  Are you there, butcher? O, I cannot speak!
CLIFFORD
  Ay, crookback, here I stand to answer thee,
  Or any he the proudest of thy sort.   97
RICHARD
  'Twas you that killed young Rutland, was it not?
CLIFFORD
  Ay, and old York, and yet not satisfied.
RICHARD
  For God's sake, lords, give signal to the fight.   100
WARWICK
  What sayst thou, Henry, wilt thou yield the crown?
QUEEN MARGARET
  Why, how now, long-tongued Warwick, dare you
    speak?
  When you and I met at Saint Albans last,
  Your legs did better service than your hands.
WARWICK
  Then 'twas my turn to fly – and now 'tis thine.
CLIFFORD
  You said so much before, and yet you fled.
WARWICK
  'Twas not your valor, Clifford, drove me thence.

---

97 *sort* gang

NORTHUMBERLAND
    No, nor your manhood that durst make you stay.
RICHARD
109   Northumberland, I hold thee reverently.
110   Break off the parley, for scarce I can refrain
111   The execution of my big-swoll'n heart
    Upon that Clifford, that cruel child-killer.
CLIFFORD
    I slew thy father – call'st thou him a child?
RICHARD
114   Ay, like a dastard and a treacherous coward,
    As thou didst kill our tender brother Rutland.
    But ere sun set I'll make thee curse the deed.
KING HENRY
    Have done with words, my lords, and hear me speak.
QUEEN MARGARET
    Defy them, then, or else hold close thy lips.
KING HENRY
    I prithee give no limits to my tongue –
120   I am a king, and privileged to speak.
CLIFFORD
    My liege, the wound that bred this meeting here
    Cannot be cured by words – therefore be still.
RICHARD
    Then, executioner, unsheathe thy sword.
124   By him that made us all, I am resolved
125   That Clifford's manhood lies upon his tongue.
EDWARD DUKE OF YORK
    Say, Henry, shall I have my right or no?
    A thousand men have broke their fasts today
    That ne'er shall dine unless thou yield the crown.
WARWICK   *To King Henry*
129   If thou deny, their blood upon thy head;

---

109 *reverently* in respect **111** *big-swoll'n* passionate **114** *dastard* coward
124 *resolved* convinced **125** *Clifford's . . . tongue* i.e., he talks better than he
fights **129** *deny* refuse

For York in justice puts his armor on.   130
PRINCE EDWARD
  If that be right which Warwick says is right,
  There is no wrong, but everything is right.
RICHARD
  Whoever got thee, there thy mother stands –   133
  For, well I wot, thou hast thy mother's tongue.   134
QUEEN MARGARET
  But thou art neither like thy sire nor dam,
  But like a foul misshapen stigmatic,   136
  Marked by the destinies to be avoided,
  As venom toads or lizards' dreadful stings.   138
RICHARD
  Iron of Naples, hid with English gilt,   139
  Whose father bears the title of a king –   140
  As if a channel should be called the sea –   141
  Sham'st thou not, knowing whence thou art extraught,   142
  To let thy tongue detect thy base-born heart?   143
EDWARD DUKE OF YORK
  A wisp of straw were worth a thousand crowns   144
  To make this shameless callet know herself.   145
    To Queen Margaret
  Helen of Greece was fairer far than thou,   146
  Although thy husband may be Menelaus;
  And ne'er was Agamemnon's brother wronged
  By that false woman, as this king by thee.
  His father reveled in the heart of France,   150

---

133 *got* begot   134 *wot* know   136 *stigmatic* one branded (stigmatized) by
deformity   138 *venom* venomous   139 *Iron . . . gilt* i.e., you cheap Neapoli-
tan (Naples was known for prostitution and venereal disease), whose worth-
lessness is concealed by English gold (perhaps punning on Suffolk's "guilt"
for having paid so much for her)   141 *channel* gutter   142 *Sham'st thou not*
are you not ashamed; *extraught* descended   143 *detect* reveal   144 *wisp of
straw* (traditional mark of a scold); *were* would be   145 *callet* whore   146–
48 *Helen . . . Menelaus . . . Agamemnon* (Paris of Troy abducted Helen, wife
of Menelaus, king of Sparta, who was brother to Agamemnon, king of Myce-
nae; here Helen is the typical false woman and Menelaus the typical cuckold.
There is an allusion to the belief that Prince Edward was not the son of
Henry VI.)   150 *His father* i.e., Henry V

151 And tamed the king, and made the dauphin stoop;
152 And had he matched according to his state,
He might have kept that glory to this day.
But when he took a beggar to his bed,
155 And graced thy poor sire with his bridal day,
Even then that sunshine brewed a shower for him
157 That washed his father's fortunes forth of France,
And heaped sedition on his crown at home.
159 For what hath broached this tumult but thy pride?
160 Hadst thou been meek, our title still had slept,
And we, in pity of the gentle king,
162 Had slipped our claim until another age.

GEORGE   *To Queen Margaret*
But when we saw our sunshine made thy spring,
164 And that thy summer bred us no increase,
165 We set the ax to thy usurping root.
166 And though the edge hath something hit ourselves,
Yet know thou, since we have begun to strike,
We'll never leave till we have hewn thee down,
169 Or bathed thy growing with our heated bloods.

EDWARD DUKE OF YORK   *To Queen Margaret*
170 And in this resolution I defy thee,
Not willing any longer conference
172 Since thou deniest the gentle king to speak.
Sound trumpets – let our bloody colors wave!
And either victory, or else a grave!

QUEEN MARGARET
Stay, Edward.

EDWARD DUKE OF YORK
No, wrangling woman, we'll no longer stay –
These words will cost ten thousand lives this day.

---

151 *dauphin* (title held by the French king's eldest son)   152 *he* i.e., Henry VI; *matched* married; *state* rank   155 *graced . . . day* i.e., did honor (grace) to your lowly father by marrying you   157 *of* from   159 *broached* started (literally, set flowing)   160 *title* claim to the throne   162 *slipped* postponed   164 *increase* harvest   165 *usurping* (because she is wife to Henry VI, regarded by the Yorkists as a usurper)   166 *something* to some extent   169 *bathed* watered   172 *deniest* forbid

Flourish. March. Exeunt York and his Men at one door,
and Queen Margaret and her Men at another door.

*

∾ **II.3** *Alarum. Excursions. Enter the Earl of Warwick.*

WARWICK

Forespent with toil, as runners with a race,   1
I lay me down a little while to breathe;   2
For strokes received, and many blows repaid,
Have robbed my strong-knit sinews of their strength,   4
And, spite of spite, needs must I rest a while.   5
    Enter Edward Duke of York, running.

EDWARD DUKE OF YORK

Smile, gentle heaven, or strike, ungentle death!   6
For this world frowns, and Edward's sun is clouded.   7

WARWICK

How now, my lord, what hap? What hope of good?
    Enter George, running.

GEORGE

Our hap is loss, our hope but sad despair;   9
Our ranks are broke, and ruin follows us.   10
What counsel give you? Whither shall we fly?

EDWARD DUKE OF YORK

Bootless is flight – they follow us with wings,   12
And weak we are, and cannot shun pursuit.   13
    Enter Richard, running.

RICHARD

Ah, Warwick, why hast thou withdrawn thyself?
Thy brother's blood the thirsty earth hath drunk,   15
Broached with the steely point of Clifford's lance.   16

II.3 Fields near York s.d. *Alarum* a trumpet call meaning "to arms"; *Excursions* attacks and counterattacks **1** *Forespent* exhausted **2** *breathe* rest **4** *strong-knit* powerful **5** *spite of spite* come what may **6** *ungentle* ignoble **7** *sun* i.e., good fortune (with allusion to the Yorkists' sun device) **9** *hap* luck **12** *Bootless* hopeless **13** *shun* avoid **15** *Thy brother's blood* (a reference to the "Bastard of Salisbury," Warwick's half brother, killed at Ferrybridge) **16** *Broached* set flowing

And in the very pangs of death he cried,
Like to a dismal clangor heard from far,
"Warwick, revenge – brother, revenge my death!"
20 So, underneath the belly of their steeds
21 That stained their fetlocks in his smoking blood,
The noble gentleman gave up the ghost.

WARWICK
Then let the earth be drunken with our blood.
I'll kill my horse, because I will not fly.
Why stand we like softhearted women here,
26 Wailing our losses, whiles the foe doth rage,
27 And look upon, as if the tragedy
Were played in jest by counterfeiting actors?
    Kneeling
Here, on my knee, I vow to God above
30 I'll never pause again, never stand still,
Till either death hath closed these eyes of mine
Or fortune given me measure of revenge.

EDWARD DUKE OF YORK   *Kneeling*
O, Warwick, I do bend my knee with thine,
And in this vow do chain my soul to thine.
And, ere my knee rise from the earth's cold face,
36 I throw my hands, mine eyes, my heart to thee,
Thou setter up and plucker down of kings,
38 Beseeching thee, if with thy will it stands
That to my foes this body must be prey,
40 Yet that thy brazen gates of heaven may ope
And give sweet passage to my sinful soul.
    They rise.
Now, lords, take leave until we meet again,
Where'er it be, in heaven or in earth.

RICHARD
44 Brother, give me thy hand; and, gentle Warwick,
Let me embrace thee in my weary arms.
I, that did never weep, now melt with woe

---

21 *smoking* steaming   26 *whiles* while   27 *upon* on   36 *thee* i.e., God   38 *stands* agrees   44 *gentle* noble

That winter should cut off our springtime so.
WARWICK
  Away, away! Once more, sweet lords, farewell.
GEORGE
  Yet let us all together to our troops,
  And give them leave to fly that will not stay;   50
  And call them pillars that will stand to us;   51
  And, if we thrive, promise them such rewards
  As victors wear at the Olympian games.
  This may plant courage in their quailing breasts,
  For yet is hope of life and victory.
  Forslow no longer – make we hence amain.   *Exeunt.* 56

                       ✳

⌘ **II.4** *Alarums. Excursions. Enter Richard at one door*
     and Lord Clifford at the other.

RICHARD
  Now, Clifford, I have singled thee alone.   1
  Suppose this arm is for the Duke of York,
  And this for Rutland, both bound to revenge,
  Wert thou environed with a brazen wall.   4
CLIFFORD
  Now, Richard, I am with thee here alone.
  This is the hand that stabbed thy father York,
  And this the hand that slew thy brother Rutland,
  And here's the heart that triumphs in their death
  And cheers these hands that slew thy sire and brother
  To execute the like upon thyself –   10
  And so, have at thee!
    They fight. The Earl of Warwick comes and rescues
    Richard. Lord Clifford flies.
RICHARD
  Nay, Warwick, single out some other chase –   12
  For I myself will hunt this wolf to death.   *Exeunt.*

---

50 *leave* permission 51 *to* by 56 *Forslow* delay; *amain* quickly
   II.4 Fields near York 1 *singled* i.e., chosen one from the herd (a hunting term)
4 *environed* surrounded 12 *chase* prey

*

∾ **II.5** *Alarum. Enter King Henry.*

KING HENRY
    This battle fares like to the morning's war,
        When dying clouds contend with growing light,
3   What time the shepherd, blowing of his nails,
        Can neither call it perfect day nor night.
    Now sways it this way like a mighty sea
        Forced by the tide to combat with the wind,
    Now sways it that way like the selfsame sea
        Forced to retire by fury of the wind.
    Sometime the flood prevails, and then the wind;
10   Now one the better, then another best –
    Both tugging to be victors, breast to breast,
    Yet neither conqueror nor conquerèd.
13   So is the equal poise of this fell war.
14   Here on this molehill will I sit me down.
    To whom God will, there be the victory.
    For Margaret my queen, and Clifford, too,
    Have chid me from the battle, swearing both
    They prosper best of all when I am thence.
    Would I were dead, if God's good will were so –
20   For what is in this world but grief and woe?
    O God! Methinks it were a happy life
22   To be no better than a homely swain.
    To sit upon a hill, as I do now;
24   To carve out dials quaintly, point by point,
    Thereby to see the minutes how they run:
    How many makes the hour full complete,
27   How many hours brings about the day,
    How many days will finish up the year,

II.5 *Fields near York* **3** *What time* when; *of* on (for warmth) **13** *poise* balance; *fell* cruel **14** *molehill* (see the note to I.4.68) **22** *homely* simple; *swain* countryman **24** *dials quaintly* sundials artfully (perhaps alluding to shepherds' practice of cutting sundials in the turf of hillsides) **27** *brings about* completes

How many years a mortal man may live.
When this is known, then to divide the times: 30
So many hours must I tend my flock,
So many hours must I take my rest,
So many hours must I contemplate,   33
So many hours must I sport myself,   34
So many days my ewes have been with young,
So many weeks ere the poor fools will ean,   36
So many years ere I shall shear the fleece.
So minutes, hours, days, weeks, months, and years,
Passed over to the end they were created,   39
Would bring white hairs unto a quiet grave.   40
Ah, what a life were this! How sweet! How lovely!
Gives not the hawthorn bush a sweeter shade
To shepherds looking on their seely sheep   43
Than doth a rich embroidered canopy
To kings that fear their subjects' treachery?
O yes, it doth – a thousandfold it doth.
And to conclude, the shepherd's homely curds,
His cold thin drink out of his leather bottle,
His wonted sleep under a fresh tree's shade,   49
All which secure and sweetly he enjoys,   50
Is far beyond a prince's delicates,   51
His viands sparkling in a golden cup,   52
His body couchèd in a curious bed,   53
When care, mistrust, and treason waits on him.   54
    Alarum. Enter at one door a Lancastrian Soldier with
    a dead Yorkist Soldier in his arms. Henry stands apart.
LANCASTRIAN SOLDIER
    Ill blows the wind that profits nobody.
    This man, whom hand to hand I slew in fight,
    May be possessèd with some store of crowns;   57

---

33 *contemplate* meditate, pray   34 *sport* amuse   36 *ean* give birth   39 *end
they* end for which they   43 *seely* innocent   49 *wonted* accustomed   51 *delicates* dainty foods   52 *viands* food   53 *curious* (1) elaborately wrought, (2)
full of cares   54 s.d. *Lancastrian . . . Yorkist* (we know these allegiances from
ll. 64–66, but the characters were probably visually identifiable to the audience at this point by their costumes)   57 *crowns* money

58 And I, that haply take them from him now,
    May yet ere night yield both my life and them
60 To some man else, as this dead man doth me.
        He removes the dead man's helmet.
    Who's this? O God! It is my father's face
62 Whom in this conflict I, unwares, have killed.
63 O, heavy times, begetting such events!
64 From London by the king was I pressed forth;
65 My father, being the Earl of Warwick's man,
66 Came on the part of York, pressed by his master;
    And I, who at his hands received my life,
    Have by my hands of life bereavèd him.
    Pardon me, God, I knew not what I did;
70 And pardon, father, for I knew not thee.
    My tears shall wipe away these bloody marks,
    And no more words till they have flowed their fill.
        He weeps.
KING HENRY
    O piteous spectacle! O bloody times!
    Whiles lions war and battle for their dens,
75 Poor harmless lambs abide their enmity.
    Weep, wretched man, I'll aid thee tear for tear;
    And let our hearts and eyes, like civil war,
78 Be blind with tears, and break, o'ercharged with grief.
        *Enter at another door another Soldier with a dead
        man in his arms.*
SECOND SOLDIER
    Thou that so stoutly hath resisted me,
80 Give me thy gold, if thou hast any gold –
    For I have bought it with an hundred blows.
        He removes the dead man's helmet.
82 But let me see: is this our foeman's face?

---

58 *haply* by chance **62** *unwares* unknowingly **63** *heavy* miserable **64** *pressed* impressed, drafted (into service against my will) **65** *man* servant **66** *part* side **75** *abide* endure **78** *o'ercharged* overfilled; s.d. *Soldier . . . dead man* (In so formal a scene as this, one would expect this second pair to reverse the allegiances of the first: here, a Yorkist soldier carrying a dead Lancastrian soldier. But here the text provides no evidence.) **82** *foeman's* enemy's

Ah, no, no, no – it is mine only son!
Ah, boy, if any life be left in thee,
Throw up thine eye! *(Weeping)* See, see, what showers
  arise,
Blown with the windy tempest of my heart,
Upon thy wounds, that kills mine eye and heart!
O, pity, God, this miserable age!
What stratagems, how fell, how butcherly,   89
Erroneous, mutinous, and unnatural,   90
This deadly quarrel daily doth beget!
O boy, thy father gave thee life too soon,
And hath bereft thee of thy life too late!   93

KING HENRY
Woe above woe! Grief more than common grief!
O that my death would stay these ruthful deeds!   95
O, pity, pity, gentle heaven, pity!
The red rose and the white are on his face,
The fatal colors of our striving houses;
The one his purple blood right well resembles,
The other his pale cheeks, methinks, presenteth.   100
Wither one rose, and let the other flourish –
If you contend, a thousand lives must wither.

LANCASTRIAN SOLDIER
How will my mother for a father's death
Take on with me, and ne'er be satisfied!   104

SECOND SOLDIER
How will my wife for slaughter of my son
Shed seas of tears, and ne'er be satisfied!

KING HENRY
How will the country for these woeful chances   107
Misthink the king, and not be satisfied!   108

LANCASTRIAN SOLDIER
Was ever son so rued a father's death?

---

89 *stratagems* bloody acts; *fell* cruel   90 *Erroneous* criminal   93 *late* recently
95 *stay* stop; *ruthful* pitiful   100 *presenteth* symbolizes   104 *Take on with*
rage against; *satisfied* comforted   107 *chances* happenings   108 *Misthink*
misunderstand, blame

SECOND SOLDIER

110 Was ever father so bemoaned his son?

KING HENRY

Was ever king so grieved for subjects' woe?

Much is your sorrow, mine ten times so much.

LANCASTRIAN SOLDIER *To his father's body*

I'll bear thee hence where I may weep my fill.

                    Exit at one door with the body of his father.

SECOND SOLDIER *To his son's body*

114 These arms of mine shall be thy winding-sheet;

My heart, sweet boy, shall be thy sepulcher,

For from my heart thine image ne'er shall go.

My sighing breast shall be thy funeral bell,

118 And so obsequious will thy father be,

E'en for the loss of thee, having no more,

120 As Priam was for all his valiant sons.

I'll bear thee hence, and let them fight that will –

For I have murdered where I should not kill.

                    Exit at another door with the body of his son.

KING HENRY

123 Sad-hearted men, much overgone with care,

Here sits a king more woeful than you are.

      Alarums. Excursions. Enter Prince Edward.

PRINCE EDWARD

Fly, father, fly – for all your friends are fled,

126 And Warwick rages like a chafèd bull!

Away – for death doth hold us in pursuit!

      Enter Queen Margaret.

QUEEN MARGARET

128 Mount you, my lord – towards Berwick post amain.

129 Edward and Richard, like a brace of greyhounds

130 Having the fearful flying hare in sight,

---

114 *winding-sheet* shroud 118 *obsequious* dutiful in mourning 120 *Priam* king of Troy (whose fifty sons were killed defending the city) 123 *overgone* overcome 126 *chafèd* angry 128 *Berwick* Berwick-on-Tweed, in Northumberland; *post* ride; *amain* at full speed 129 *brace* pair

With fiery eyes sparkling for very wrath,
And bloody steel grasped in their ireful hands,
Are at our backs – and therefore hence amain.
   Enter Exeter.

EXETER
Away – for vengeance comes along with them!
Nay – stay not to expostulate – make speed –   135
Or else come after. I'll away before.

KING HENRY
Nay, take me with thee, good sweet Exeter.
Not that I fear to stay, but love to go
Whither the queen intends. Forward, away.   *Exeunt.*

*

∾ **II.6** *A loud alarum. Enter Lord Clifford, wounded
with an arrow in his neck.*

CLIFFORD
Here burns my candle out – ay, here it dies,
Which, whiles it lasted, gave King Henry light.   2
O Lancaster, I fear thy overthrow   3
More than my body's parting with my soul!
My love and fear glued many friends to thee –   5
And, now I fall, thy tough commixture melts,   6
Impairing Henry, strength'ning misproud York.   7
The common people swarm like summer flies,
And whither fly the gnats but to the sun?   9
And who shines now but Henry's enemies?   *10*
O Phoebus, hadst thou never given consent   11
That Phaëthon should check thy fiery steeds,   12
Thy burning car never had scorched the earth!   13

---

135 *expostulate* argue
   II.6 Fields near York 2 *whiles* while 3 *Lancaster* i.e., the house of Lancaster 5 *My . . . fear* the love and respect I commanded 6 *commixture* compound 7 *Impairing* weakening; *misproud* unjustly proud 9 *sun* (another allusion to the Yorkist sun device) 11 *Phoebus* Phoebus Apollo, the sun 12 *Phaëthon* (see the note to I.4.34); *check* manage 13 *car* chariot

14 And, Henry, hadst thou swayed as kings should do,
    Or as thy father and his father did,
    Giving no ground unto the house of York,
17 They never then had sprung like summer flies;
    I and ten thousand in this luckless realm
    Had left no mourning widows for our death;
20 And thou this day hadst kept thy chair in peace.
21 For what doth cherish weeds, but gentle air?
    And what makes robbers bold, but too much lenity?
23 Bootless are plaints, and cureless are my wounds;
    No way to fly, nor strength to hold out flight;
    The foe is merciless and will not pity,
    For at their hands I have deserved no pity.
    The air hath got into my deadly wounds,
28 And much effuse of blood doth make me faint.
    Come York and Richard, Warwick and the rest –
30 I stabbed your fathers' bosoms; split my breast.
        He faints.
        Alarum and retreat. Enter Edward Duke of York,
        his brothers George and Richard, the Earl of Warwick,
        the Marquis of Montague, and Soldiers.
EDWARD DUKE OF YORK
    Now breathe we, lords – good fortune bids us pause,
    And smooth the frowns of war with peaceful looks.
    Some troops pursue the bloody-minded queen,
    That led calm Henry, though he were a king,
35 As doth a sail filled with a fretting gust
36 Command an argosy to stem the waves.
    But think you, lords, that Clifford fled with them?
WARWICK
    No – 'tis impossible he should escape;
    For, though before his face I speak the words,
40 Your brother Richard marked him for the grave.

---

14 *swayed* ruled   17 *sprung* multiplied   20 *chair* i.e., of state, throne   21
cherish foster   23 *Bootless* useless; *plaints* pleas   28 *effuse* effusion   30 s.d.
retreat a trumpet call signaling recall   35 *fretting* (1) blowing in gusts, (2)
nagging   36 *argosy* large merchant ship; *stem* resist

And wheresoe'er he is, he's surely dead.
   Clifford groans.

EDWARD DUKE OF YORK
Whose soul is that which takes her heavy leave?

RICHARD
A deadly groan, like life and death's departing.

EDWARD DUKE OF YORK   *To Richard*
See who it is.
   Richard goes to Clifford.
        And now the battle's ended,
If friend or foe, let him be gently used.

RICHARD
Revoke that doom of mercy, for 'tis Clifford;   46
Who not contented that he lopped the branch
In hewing Rutland when his leaves put forth,
But set his murd'ring knife unto the root
From whence that tender spray did sweetly spring –   50
I mean our princely father, Duke of York.

WARWICK
From off the gates of York fetch down the head,
Your father's head, which Clifford placèd there.
Instead whereof let this *(Indicating Clifford's head)* sup-   54
  ply the room –
Measure for measure must be answerèd.   55

EDWARD DUKE OF YORK
Bring forth that fatal screech owl to our house,   56
That nothing sung but death to us and ours.
   Clifford is dragged forward.
Now death shall stop his dismal threat'ning sound
And his ill-boding tongue no more shall speak.   59

WARWICK
I think his understanding is bereft.   60

---

46 *doom* judgment   50 *spray* shoot   54 *supply the room* take its place   55
Measure for measure i.e., the strict rule of justice that demands "an eye for an
eye" (the allusion is to the New Testament, however: Mark 4:24); *answerèd*
given in reply   56 *fatal . . . house* doom-prophesying bird whose predictions
are directed particularly at our family   59 *ill-boding* doom-promising   60
understanding consciousness; *bereft* lost

Speak, Clifford, dost thou know who speaks to thee?
Dark cloudy death o'ershades his beams of life,
63   And he nor sees nor hears us what we say.

RICHARD

O, would he did – and so perhaps he doth.
65   'Tis but his policy to counterfeit,
Because he would avoid such bitter taunts
Which in the time of death he gave our father.

GEORGE

68   If so thou think'st, vex him with eager words.

RICHARD

Clifford, ask mercy and obtain no grace.

EDWARD DUKE OF YORK

70   Clifford, repent in bootless penitence.

WARWICK

Clifford, devise excuses for thy faults.

GEORGE

72   While we devise fell tortures for thy faults.

RICHARD

Thou didst love York, and I am son to York.

EDWARD DUKE OF YORK

Thou pitied'st Rutland – I will pity thee.

GEORGE

75   Where's Captain Margaret to fence you now?

WARWICK

76   They mock thee, Clifford – swear as thou wast wont.

RICHARD

What, not an oath? Nay, then, the world goes hard
When Clifford cannot spare his friends an oath.
I know by that he's dead – and, by my soul,
80   If this right hand would buy but two hours' life
That I, in all despite, might rail at him,
    Raising his left hand
This hand should chop it off, and with the issuing
blood

---

63 *nor . . . nor* neither . . . nor   65 *policy* stratagem   68 *eager* bitter   72 *fell*
cruel   75 *fence* protect   76 *wont* accustomed

Stifle the villain whose unstanchèd thirst   83
York and young Rutland could not satisfy.

WARWICK
Ay, but he's dead. Off with the traitor's head,
And rear it in the place your father's stands.
And now to London with triumphant march,
There to be crownèd England's royal king;
From whence shall Warwick cut the sea to France,
And ask the Lady Bonnë for thy queen.   90
So shalt thou sinew both these lands together.   91
And, having France thy friend, thou shalt not dread
The scattered foe that hopes to rise again,
For though they cannot greatly sting to hurt,
Yet look to have them buzz to offend thine ears.   95
First will I see the coronation,
And then to Brittany I'll cross the sea
To effect this marriage, so it please my lord.

EDWARD DUKE OF YORK
Even as thou wilt, sweet Warwick, let it be.
For in thy shoulder do I build my seat,   100
And never will I undertake the thing
Wherein thy counsel and consent is wanting.
Richard, I will create thee Duke of Gloucester,
And George, of Clarence; Warwick, as ourself,
Shall do and undo as him pleaseth best.

RICHARD
Let me be Duke of Clarence, George of Gloucester –
For Gloucester's dukedom is too ominous.   107

WARWICK
Tut, that's a foolish observation –   108

---

83 *Stifle* strangle; *unstanchèd* unquenchable   91 *sinew* join (as if tied with
sinew)   95 *buzz* circulate scandal   100 *in thy shoulder* with your support
107 *too ominous* (because the three immediately preceding dukes of Gloucester had died violent deaths)   108 *observation* comment

Richard, be Duke of Gloucester. Now to London
110   To see these honors in possession.
    Exeunt. Richard late Duke of York's head is removed.

       *

 ❧ **III.1** *Enter two Gamekeepers, with crossbows in their
  hands.*

FIRST GAMEKEEPER
1 Under this thick-grown brake we'll shroud ourselves,
2 For through this laund anon the deer will come,
 And in this covert will we make our stand,
4 Culling the principal of all the deer.
SECOND GAMEKEEPER
 I'll stay above the hill, so both may shoot.
FIRST GAMEKEEPER
 That cannot be – the noise of thy crossbow
7 Will scare the herd, and so my shoot is lost.
8 Here stand we both, and aim we at the best.
9 And, for the time shall not seem tedious,
10 I'll tell thee what befell me on a day
11 In this self place where now we mean to stand.
FIRST GAMEKEEPER
 Here comes a man – let's stay till he be past.
  They stand apart.
  Enter King Henry, disguised, carrying a prayer book.
KING HENRY
13 From Scotland am I stolen, even of pure love,
14 To greet mine own land with my wishful sight.
 No, Harry, Harry – 'tis no land of thine.
 Thy place is filled, thy scepter wrung from thee,
 Thy balm washed off wherewith thou wast anointed.

---

110 s.d. *removed* (Clifford's head may for a while be displayed in its place,
but for how long it is impossible to know)
 III.1 A forest in northern England, near the Scottish border **1** *brake*
thicket **2** *laund* glade **4** *Culling* selecting; *principal* best **7** *shoot* discharge
of arrows **8** *at the best* as well as we can **9** *for* so that **11** *self* same
13 *even of* precisely because of **14** *wishful* longing

No bending knee will call thee Caesar now,
No humble suitors press to speak for right,   19
No, not a man comes for redress of thee –   20
For how can I help them and not myself?

FIRST GAMEKEEPER   *To the Second Gamekeeper*
Ay, here's a deer whose skin's a keeper's fee: 22
This is the quondam king – let's seize upon him.   23

KING HENRY
Let me embrace thee, sour adversity,
For wise men say it is the wisest course.   25

SECOND GAMEKEEPER   *To the First Gamekeeper*
Why linger we? Let us lay hands upon him.

FIRST GAMEKEEPER   *To the Second Gamekeeper*
Forbear awhile – we'll hear a little more.

KING HENRY
My queen and son are gone to France for aid,
And, as I hear, the great commanding Warwick
Is thither gone to crave the French king's sister   30
To wife for Edward. If this news be true,
Poor queen and son, your labor is but lost –
For Warwick is a subtle orator,
And Louis a prince soon won with moving words.
By this account, then, Margaret may win him –
For she's a woman to be pitied much.
Her sighs will make a batt'ry in his breast,   37
Her tears will pierce into a marble heart,
The tiger will be mild whiles she doth mourn,
And Nero will be tainted with remorse   40
To hear and see her plaints, her brinish tears.   41
Ay, but she's come to beg; Warwick to give.
She on his left side, craving aid for Henry;
He on his right, asking a wife for Edward.
She weeps and says her Henry is deposed,

---

19 *speak for right* beg for justice **20** *of* from **22** *fee* i.e., perquisite of the job of gamekeeper **23** *quondam* former **25** *it* i.e., accepting adversity **37** *batt'ry* breach **40** *Nero* (traditionally hardhearted and cruel); *tainted* affected **41** *plaints* pleas; *brinish* salty

He smiles and says his Edward is installed;
47 That she, poor wretch, for grief can speak no more,
48 Whiles Warwick tells his title, smooths the wrong,
49 Inferreth arguments of mighty strength,
50 And in conclusion wins the king from her
51 With promise of his sister and what else
　　To strengthen and support King Edward's place.
　　O, Margaret, thus 'twill be; and thou, poor soul,
　　Art then forsaken, as thou went'st forlorn.
SECOND GAMEKEEPER *Coming forward*
　　Say, what art thou that talk'st of kings and queens?
KING HENRY
　　More than I seem, and less than I was born to:
　　A man at least, for less I should not be;
　　And men may talk of kings, and why not I?
SECOND GAMEKEEPER
　　Ay, but thou talk'st as if thou wert a king.
KING HENRY
60 Why, so I am, in mind – and that's enough.
SECOND GAMEKEEPER
　　But if thou be a king, where is thy crown?
KING HENRY
　　My crown is in my heart, not on my head;
63 Not decked with diamonds and Indian stones,
　　Nor to be seen. My crown is called content –
　　A crown it is that seldom kings enjoy.
SECOND GAMEKEEPER
　　Well, if you be a king crowned with content,
　　Your crown content and you must be contented
　　To go along with us – for, as we think,
　　You are the king King Edward hath deposed,
70 And we his subjects sworn in all allegiance
　　Will apprehend you as his enemy.

---

47 *That* so that 48 *tells his title* explains Edward's claim to the throne; *smooths* glosses over 49 *Inferreth* adduces 51 *and what else* i.e., and who knows what other promises 63 *Indian stones* gems (probably pearls)

KING HENRY
  But did you never swear and break an oath?
SECOND GAMEKEEPER
  No – never such an oath, nor will not now.
KING HENRY
  Where did you dwell when I was King of England?
SECOND GAMEKEEPER
  Here in this country, where we now remain.
KING HENRY
  I was anointed king at nine months old,
  My father and my grandfather were kings,
  And you were sworn true subjects unto me –
  And tell me, then, have you not broke your oaths?
FIRST GAMEKEEPER
  No, for we were subjects but while you were king.   80
KING HENRY
  Why, am I dead? Do I not breathe a man?
  Ah, simple men, you know not what you swear.
  Look as I blow this feather from my face,
  And as the air blows it to me again,
  Obeying with my wind when I do blow,   85
  And yielding to another when it blows,
  Commanded always by the greater gust –
  Such is the lightness of you common men.   88
  But do not break your oaths, for of that sin
  My mild entreaty shall not make you guilty.   90
  Go where you will, the king shall be commanded;
  And be you kings, command, and I'll obey.
FIRST GAMEKEEPER
  We are true subjects to the king, King Edward.
KING HENRY
  So would you be again to Henry,
  If he were seated as King Edward is.
FIRST GAMEKEEPER
  We charge you, in God's name and in the king's,
  To go with us unto the officers.

―――――

80 *but* only   85 *Obeying with* submitting to   88 *lightness* fickleness

KING HENRY
    In God's name, lead; your king's name be obeyed;
    And what God will, that let your king perform;
100   And what he will I humbly yield unto.   *Exeunt.*

                                    *

∾ **III.2** *Enter King Edward, Richard Duke of*
    Gloucester, George Duke of Clarence, and Elizabeth
    Lady Grey.

KING EDWARD
    Brother of Gloucester, at Saint Albans field
2   This lady's husband, Sir Richard Grey, was slain,
    His lands then seized on by the conqueror.
    Her suit is now to repossess those lands,
    Which we in justice cannot well deny,
    Because in quarrel of the house of York
    The worthy gentleman did lose his life.
RICHARD DUKE OF GLOUCESTER
    Your highness shall do well to grant her suit –
    It were dishonor to deny it her.
KING EDWARD
10   It were no less; but yet I'll make a pause.
RICHARD DUKE OF GLOUCESTER   *Aside to George*
    Yea, is it so?
12   I see the lady hath a thing to grant
    Before the king will grant her humble suit.
GEORGE DUKE OF CLARENCE   *Aside to Richard*
14   He knows the game; how true he keeps the wind!
RICHARD DUKE OF GLOUCESTER   *Aside to George*
    Silence.

III.2 The palace, London   2 *Sir Richard Grey* (Lady Grey's husband, actually
Sir John, was killed at the second battle of Saint Albans, where he fought the
Lancastrians. The facts are given correctly in *Richard III*, 1.3.126–29.)   12 *a
thing* (1) a favor, (2) genitals   14 *knows the game* understands the nature of
his prey (Lady Grey) (Richard and George's commentary is couched in the
language of hunting and dueling; their meaning, sexual); *keeps the wind*
hunts downwind, so as not to alarm his prey

KING EDWARD   *To Lady Grey*
  Widow, we will consider of your suit;
  And come some other time to know our mind.
ELIZABETH LADY GREY
  Right gracious lord, I cannot brook delay.   18
  May it please your highness to resolve me now,   19
  And what your pleasure is shall satisfy me.   20
RICHARD DUKE OF GLOUCESTER   *Aside to George*
  Ay, widow? Then I'll warrant you all your lands   21
  An if what pleases him shall pleasure you.   22
  Fight closer, or, good faith, you'll catch a blow.   23
GEORGE DUKE OF CLARENCE   *Aside to Richard*
  I fear her not unless she chance to fall.   24
RICHARD DUKE OF GLOUCESTER   *Aside to George*
  God forbid that! For he'll take vantages.   25
KING EDWARD   *To Lady Grey*
  How many children hast thou, widow? Tell me.
GEORGE DUKE OF CLARENCE   *Aside to Richard*
  I think he means to beg a child of her.   27
RICHARD DUKE OF GLOUCESTER   *Aside to George*
  Nay, whip me then – he'll rather give her two.   28
ELIZABETH LADY GREY   *To King Edward*
  Three, my most gracious lord.
RICHARD DUKE OF GLOUCESTER   *Aside*
  You shall have four, an you'll be ruled by him.   30
KING EDWARD   *To Lady Grey*
  'Twere pity they should lose their father's lands.
ELIZABETH LADY GREY
  Be pitiful, dread lord, and grant it them.

---

18 *brook* endure   19 *resolve me* free me from uncertainty   20 *pleasure* (1) will, (2) (sexual) desire   21 *warrant* guarantee   22 *An if* if   23 *Fight . . . blow* fight more closely to avoid his thrusts (playing on the sense of "sexual thrust")   24 *fear* fear for; *fall* (1) stumble, (2) submit to sex   25 *vantages* opportunities   27 *beg . . . her* (1) apply to her for a wardship, a source of profit if the child were highborn; (2) ask her to bear him a child   28 *whip me* (a mild imprecation; or, perhaps, literally, for being so childish as to think so)   30 *an if*

KING EDWARD   *To Richard and George*

33   Lords, give us leave – I'll try this widow's wit.

RICHARD DUKE OF GLOUCESTER   *Aside to George*

34   Ay, good leave have you; for you will have leave,

35   Till youth take leave and leave you to the crutch.
       Richard and George stand apart.

KING EDWARD   *To Lady Grey*
       Now tell me, madam, do you love your children?

ELIZABETH LADY GREY
       Ay, full as dearly as I love myself.

KING EDWARD
       And would you not do much to do them good?

ELIZABETH LADY GREY
       To do them good I would sustain some harm.

KING EDWARD

40   Then get your husband's lands, to do them good.

ELIZABETH LADY GREY
       Therefore I came unto your majesty.

KING EDWARD
       I'll tell you how these lands are to be got.

ELIZABETH LADY GREY
       So shall you bind me to your highness' service.

KING EDWARD

44   What service wilt thou do me, if I give them?

ELIZABETH LADY GREY
       What you command, that rests in me to do.

KING EDWARD

46   But you will take exceptions to my boon.

ELIZABETH LADY GREY

47   No, gracious lord, except I cannot do it.

KING EDWARD
       Ay, but thou canst do what I mean to ask.

---

33 *give us leave* pardon us (i.e., please go away)   34 *good leave* willing pardon; *have leave* take liberties   35 *take leave* bid farewell; *leave you to* pass you on to (because you will be too old to be amorous); *crutch* (playing on the sexual sense, "crotch")   44 *service* (1) duty, (2) sexual attention   46 *boon* request   47 *except* unless

ELIZABETH LADY GREY
  Why, then, I will do what your grace commands.
RICHARD DUKE OF GLOUCESTER   *To George*
  He plies her hard, and much rain wears the marble.   50
GEORGE DUKE OF CLARENCE
  As red as fire! Nay, then her wax must melt.
ELIZABETH LADY GREY   *To King Edward*
  Why stops my lord? Shall I not hear my task?
KING EDWARD
  An easy task – 'tis but to love a king.
ELIZABETH LADY GREY
  That's soon performed, because I am a subject.
KING EDWARD
  Why, then, thy husband's lands I freely give thee.
ELIZABETH LADY GREY   *Curtsies.*
  I take my leave, with many thousand thanks.
RICHARD DUKE OF GLOUCESTER   *To George*
  The match is made – she seals it with a curtsy.
KING EDWARD   *To Lady Grey*
  But stay thee – 'tis the fruits of love I mean.
ELIZABETH LADY GREY
  The fruits of love *I* mean, my loving liege.
KING EDWARD
  Ay, but I fear me in another sense.   60
  What love think'st thou I sue so much to get?
ELIZABETH LADY GREY
  My love till death, my humble thanks, my prayers –
  That love which virtue begs and virtue grants.
KING EDWARD
  No, by my troth, I did not mean such love.
ELIZABETH LADY GREY
  Why, then, you mean not as I thought you did.
KING EDWARD
  But now you partly may perceive my mind.

---

50 *plies* urges

ELIZABETH LADY GREY
  My mind will never grant what I perceive
68 Your highness aims at, if I aim aright.
KING EDWARD
  To tell thee plain, I aim to lie with thee.
ELIZABETH LADY GREY
70 To tell *you* plain, I had rather lie in prison.
KING EDWARD
  Why, then, thou shalt not have thy husband's lands.
ELIZABETH LADY GREY
72 Why, then, mine honesty shall be my dower;
  For by that loss I will not purchase them.
KING EDWARD
  Therein thou wrong'st thy children mightily.
ELIZABETH LADY GREY
  Herein your highness wrongs both them and me.
  But, mighty lord, this merry inclination
77 Accords not with the sadness of my suit.
  Please you dismiss me either with ay or no.
KING EDWARD
  Ay, if thou wilt say "ay" to my request;
80 No, if thou dost say "no" to my demand.
ELIZABETH LADY GREY
  Then, no, my lord – my suit is at an end.
RICHARD DUKE OF GLOUCESTER   *To George*
  The widow likes him not – she knits her brows.
GEORGE DUKE OF CLARENCE
  He is the bluntest wooer in Christendom.
KING EDWARD   *Aside*
84 Her looks doth argue her replete with modesty;
  Her words doth show her wit incomparable;
86 All her perfections challenge sovereignty.
  One way or other, she is for a king;
  And she shall be my love or else my queen.

---

68 *aim* guess; *aright* correctly   **72** *honesty* honor   **77** *sadness* seriousness   **84** *argue* prove   **86** *challenge* lay claim to

To Lady Grey
Say that King Edward take thee for his queen?

ELIZABETH LADY GREY
'Tis better said than done, my gracious lord.   *90*
I am a subject fit to jest withal,
But far unfit to be a sovereign.

KING EDWARD
Sweet widow, by my state I swear to thee   *93*
I speak no more than what my soul intends,
And that is to enjoy thee for my love.

ELIZABETH LADY GREY
And that is more than I will yield unto.
I know I am too mean to be your queen,
And yet too good to be your concubine.

KING EDWARD
You cavil, widow – I did mean my queen.   *99*

ELIZABETH LADY GREY
'Twill grieve your grace my sons should call you father.   *100*

KING EDWARD
No more than when my daughters call thee mother.
Thou art a widow and thou hast some children;
And, by God's mother, I, being but a bachelor,
Have other some. Why, 'tis a happy thing   *104*
To be the father unto many sons.
Answer no more, for thou shalt be my queen.

RICHARD DUKE OF GLOUCESTER   *To George*
The ghostly father now hath done his shrift.   *107*

GEORGE DUKE OF CLARENCE
When he was made a shriver, 'twas for shift.   *108*

KING EDWARD   *To Richard and George*
Brothers, you muse what chat we two have had.   *109*

---

93 *state* kingship   **99** *cavil* quibble frivolously   **104** *other some* some others
107 *ghostly* spiritual; *father* i.e., a priest; *done his shrift* finished hearing confession   **108** *for shift* (1) as a trick to serve some purpose, (2) to gain access to her undergarments (to say that a woman was "shriven to her shift" was a common off-color joke meaning that she had been seduced)   **109** *muse* wonder

Richard and George come forward.

RICHARD DUKE OF GLOUCESTER

110   The widow likes it not, for she looks very sad.

KING EDWARD

You'd think it strange if I should marry her.

GEORGE DUKE OF CLARENCE

To who, my lord?

KING EDWARD   Why, Clarence, to myself.

RICHARD DUKE OF GLOUCESTER

113   That would be ten days' wonder at the least.

GEORGE DUKE OF CLARENCE

That's a day longer than a wonder lasts.

RICHARD DUKE OF GLOUCESTER

115   By so much is the wonder in extremes.

KING EDWARD

Well, jest on, brothers – I can tell you both

Her suit is granted for her husband's lands.

Enter a Nobleman.

NOBLEMAN

My gracious lord, Henry your foe is taken

And brought as prisoner to your palace gate.

KING EDWARD

120   See that he be conveyed unto the Tower –

To Richard and George

And go we, brothers, to the man that took him,

122   To question of his apprehension.

To Lady Grey

Widow, go you along. *(To Richard and George)* Lords,

use her honorably.   *Exeunt all but Richard.*

RICHARD DUKE OF GLOUCESTER

Ay, Edward will use women honorably.

125   Would he were wasted, marrow, bones, and all,

That from his loins no hopeful branch may spring

---

110 *sad* serious   113 *ten days' wonder* i.e., a most marvelous thing (proverbially, a novelty attracts for only nine days)   115 *in extremes* exceedingly
great   122 *question ... apprehension* inquire about his capture   125
wasted ... all destroyed utterly by (venereal) disease

To cross me from the golden time I look for.   127
And yet, between my soul's desire and me –
The lustful Edward's title burièd –   129
Is Clarence, Henry, and his son young Edward,   *130*
And all the unlooked-for issue of their bodies,   131
To take their rooms ere I can place myself.   132
A cold premeditation for my purpose.   133
Why, then, I do but dream on sovereignty
Like one that stands upon a promontory
And spies a far-off shore where he would tread,
Wishing his foot were equal with his eye,   137
And chides the sea that sunders him from thence,
Saying he'll lade it dry to have his way –   139
So do I wish the crown being so far off,   140
And so I chide the means that keeps me from it,   141
And so I say I'll cut the causes off,
Flattering me with impossibilities.   143
My eye's too quick, my heart o'erweens too much,   144
Unless my hand and strength could equal them.
Well, say there is no kingdom then for Richard –
What other pleasure can the world afford?
I'll make my heaven in a lady's lap,
And deck my body in gay ornaments,
And 'witch sweet ladies with my words and looks.   150
O, miserable thought! And more unlikely
Than to accomplish twenty golden crowns.   152
Why, love forswore me in my mother's womb,   153
And, for I should not deal in her soft laws,   154
She did corrupt frail nature with some bribe
To shrink mine arm up like a withered shrub,
To make an envious mountain on my back –   157
Where sits deformity to mock my body –

---

127 *cross* keep   129 *burièd* out of the way   131 *unlooked-for* unanticipated
132 *rooms* places   133 *cold premeditation* discouraging forecast   137 *equal*
with as capable as   139 *lade* ladle   140 *wish* wish for   141 *means* obstacles
143 *me* myself   144 *o'erweens* presumes   150 *'witch* bewitch   152 *accom-*
plish obtain   153 *forswore* abandoned   154 *for* so that   157 *envious* de-
tested

To shape my legs of an unequal size,
160 To disproportion me in every part,
161 Like to a chaos, or an unlicked bear whelp
162 That carries no impression like the dam.
And am I then a man to be beloved?
O, monstrous fault, to harbor such a thought!
Then, since this earth affords no joy to me
166 But to command, to check, to o'erbear such
167 As are of better person than myself,
I'll make my heaven to dream upon the crown,
And whiles I live, t' account this world but hell,
170 Until my misshaped trunk that bears this head
171 Be round impalèd with a glorious crown.
And yet I know not how to get the crown,
173 For many lives stand between me and home.
And I – like one lost in a thorny wood,
That rends the thorns and is rent with the thorns,
Seeking a way and straying from the way,
Not knowing how to find the open air,
But toiling desperately to find it out –
Torment myself to catch the English crown.
180 And from that torment I will free myself,
Or hew my way out with a bloody ax.
Why, I can smile, and murder whiles I smile,
And cry "Content!" to that which grieves my heart,
And wet my cheeks with artificial tears,
And frame my face to all occasions.
186 I'll drown more sailors than the mermaid shall;
187 I'll slay more gazers than the basilisk;
188 I'll play the orator as well as Nestor,

---

161 *chaos* unformed mass; *unlicked bear whelp* (bear cubs were supposedly born as lumps of matter and licked into shape by their mothers) 162 *impression* shape; *dam* mother 166 *check* rebuke; *o'erbear* dominate 167 *person* appearance 171 *impalèd* encircled 173 *home* i.e., my goal 186 *mermaid* siren 187 *basilisk* fabulous serpent whose look killed the gazed-upon 188 *Nestor* the aged Greek warrior at the siege of Troy, noted for his wisdom

Deceive more slyly than Ulysses could,   189
And, like a Sinon, take another Troy.   190
I can add colors to the chameleon,
Change shapes with Proteus for advantages,   192
And set the murderous Machiavel to school.   193
Can I do this, and cannot get a crown?
Tut, were it farther off, I'll pluck it down.   *Exit.*

*

∾ **III.3** *Two chairs of state. Flourish. Enter King Louis
of France, his sister the Lady Bonne, Lord Bourbon his
admiral, Prince Edward, Queen Margaret, and the
Earl of Oxford. Louis goes up upon the state, sits, and
riseth up again.*

KING LOUIS
  Fair Queen of England, worthy Margaret,
  Sit down with us. It ill befits thy state   2
  And birth that thou shouldst stand while Louis doth sit.
QUEEN MARGARET
  No, mighty King of France, now Margaret
  Must strike her sail and learn a while to serve   5
  Where kings command. I was, I must confess,
  Great Albion's queen in former golden days,   7
  But now mischance hath trod my title down,
  And with dishonor laid me on the ground,
  Where I must take like seat unto my fortune   10
  And to my humble state conform myself.

---

189 *Ulysses* the Greek warrior, the subject of the *Odyssey*, noted for his crafti-
ness 190 *a Sinon* the Greek who persuaded the Trojans to bring the
Wooden Horse into the city 192 *Proteus* the sea deity who, when captured,
changed his shape; *for advantages* as my purpose dictates 193 *Machiavel*
Machiavelli (Italian political philosopher [1469–1527], known in England as
an advocate of guile and ruthlessness in the attainment of political objectives)
    III.3 The king's palace, France s.d. *Two* (possibly three, one each for King
Louis, Queen Margaret, and Lady Bonne) 2 *state* status 5 *strike her sail*
lower her sail (a mark of deference paid at sea to a senior) 7 *Albion's* England's

KING LOUIS
   Why, say, fair queen, whence springs this deep despair?
QUEEN MARGARET
   From such a cause as fills mine eyes with tears
   And stops my tongue, while heart is drowned in cares.
KING LOUIS
15   Whate'er it be, be thou still like thyself,
   And sit thee by our side.
     Seats her by him.
                    Yield not thy neck
   To fortune's yoke, but let thy dauntless mind
   Still ride in triumph over all mischance.
   Be plain, Queen Margaret, and tell thy grief.
20   It shall be eased if France can yield relief.
QUEEN MARGARET
   Those gracious words revive my drooping thoughts,
   And give my tongue-tied sorrows leave to speak.
   Now, therefore, be it known to noble Louis
   That Henry, sole possessor of my love,
25   Is of a king become a banished man,
26   And forced to live in Scotland a forlorn,
   While proud ambitious Edward, Duke of York,
   Usurps the regal title and the seat
   Of England's true-anointed lawful king.
30   This is the cause that I, poor Margaret,
   With this my son, Prince Edward, Henry's heir,
   Am come to crave thy just and lawful aid.
   An if thou fail us all our hope is done.
   Scotland hath will to help, but cannot help;
   Our people and our peers are both misled,
   Our treasure seized, our soldiers put to flight,
   And, as thou seest, ourselves in heavy plight.
KING LOUIS
   Renownèd queen, with patience calm the storm,

---

15 *be thou . . . thyself* i.e., behave always in a way appropriate to your great-
ness **20** *France* the king of France **25** *of* instead of **26** *forlorn* outcast

While we bethink a means to break it off.   39
QUEEN MARGARET
The more we stay, the stronger grows our foe.   40
KING LOUIS
The more I stay, the more I'll succor thee.
QUEEN MARGARET
O, but impatience waiteth on true sorrow.   42
    Enter the Earl of Warwick.
And see where comes the breeder of my sorrow.
KING LOUIS
What's he approacheth boldly to our presence?
QUEEN MARGARET
Our Earl of Warwick, Edward's greatest friend.
KING LOUIS
Welcome, brave Warwick. What brings thee to France?
    He descends. She ariseth.
QUEEN MARGARET *Aside*
Ay, now begins a second storm to rise,
For this is he that moves both wind and tide.
WARWICK   *To King Louis*
From worthy Edward, King of Albion,
My lord and sovereign, and thy vowèd friend,   50
I come in kindness and unfeignèd love,
First, to do greetings to thy royal person,
And then, to crave a league of amity,   53
And lastly, to confirm that amity
With nuptial knot, if thou vouchsafe to grant
That virtuous Lady Bonnë, thy fair sister,   56
To England's king in lawful marriage.
QUEEN MARGARET *Aside*
If that go forward, Henry's hope is done.
WARWICK   *To Lady Bonne*
And, gracious madam, in our king's behalf
I am commanded, with your leave and favor,   60

_____

39 *break it off* stop it   40 *stay* delay   42 *waiteth on* attends   53 *league* alliance; *amity* friendship   56 *sister* i.e., sister-in-law

Humbly to kiss your hand, and with my tongue
To tell the passion of my sovereign's heart,
Where fame, late ent'ring at his heedful ears,
Hath placed thy beauty's image and thy virtue.

QUEEN MARGARET
King Louis and Lady Bonnë, hear me speak
Before you answer Warwick. His demand
Springs not from Edward's well-meant honest love,
But from deceit, bred by necessity.
For how can tyrants safely govern home
70   Unless abroad they purchase great alliance?
To prove him tyrant this reason may suffice –
That Henry liveth still; but were he dead,
Yet here Prince Edward stands, King Henry's son.
Look, therefore, Louis, that by this league and marriage
Thou draw not on thy danger and dishonor,
76   For though usurpers sway the rule a while,
Yet heav'ns are just and time suppresseth wrongs.

WARWICK
78   Injurious Margaret.

PRINCE EDWARD   And why not "Queen"?

WARWICK
Because thy father Henry did usurp,
80   And thou no more art prince than she is queen.

OXFORD
81   Then Warwick disannuls great John of Ghent,
82   Which did subdue the greatest part of Spain;
And, after John of Ghent, Henry the Fourth,
Whose wisdom was a mirror to the wisest;
And, after that wise prince, Henry the Fifth,
Who by his prowess conquerèd all France.
From these our Henry lineally descends.

WARWICK
Oxford, how haps it in this smooth discourse
You told not how Henry the Sixth hath lost

---

70 *purchase* obtain   76 *sway the rule* exercise power   78 *Injurious* insulting
81 *disannuls* cancels out   82 *Which . . . Spain* (John of Ghent did campaign
in Spain, but his successes were minor)

All that which Henry the Fifth had gotten?   *90*
Methinks these peers of France should smile at that.
But for the rest, you tell a pedigree   *92*
Of threescore and two years – a silly time
To make prescription for a kingdom's worth.

OXFORD
Why, Warwick, canst thou speak against thy liege,
Whom thou obeyedest thirty and six years,
And not bewray thy treason with a blush?   *97*

WARWICK
Can Oxford, that did ever fence the right,   *98*
Now buckler falsehood with a pedigree?   *99*
For shame – leave Henry, and call Edward king.   *100*

OXFORD
Call him my king by whose injurious doom   *101*
My elder brother, the Lord Aubrey Vere,   *102*
Was done to death? And more than so, my father,   *103*
Even in the downfall of his mellowed years,   *104*
When nature brought him to the door of death?
No, Warwick, no – while life upholds this arm,
This arm upholds the house of Lancaster.

WARWICK
And I the house of York.

KING LOUIS
Queen Margaret, Prince Edward, and Oxford,
Vouchsafe, at our request, to stand aside   *110*
While I use further conference with Warwick.   *111*
    Queen Margaret comes down from the state and, with
    Prince Edward and Oxford, stands apart.

QUEEN MARGARET
Heavens grant that Warwick's words bewitch him not.

92–94 *you . . . worth* i.e., the line you describe runs for sixty-two years, a ridiculously short time upon which to base a claim sanctioned by custom (*prescription*) to the wealth and honor of kingship   97 *bewray* reveal   98 *fence the right* defend justice   99 *buckler* shield   101 *injurious doom* insulting judgment   102 *Lord Aubrey Vere* (Holinshed reports that in 1462 the twelfth Earl of Oxford and Lord Aubrey Vere, his eldest son, were accused of treason and executed)   103 *more than so* yet more   104 *downfall* decline   111 *use further conference* talk further

KING LOUIS
   Now, Warwick, tell me even upon thy conscience,
   Is Edward your true king? For I were loath
   To link with him that were not lawful chosen.
WARWICK
   Thereon I pawn my credit and mine honor.
KING LOUIS
   But is he gracious in the people's eye?
WARWICK
   The more that Henry was unfortunate.
KING LOUIS
   Then further, all dissembling set aside,
120   Tell me for truth the measure of his love
   Unto our sister Bonnë.
WARWICK   Such it seems
122   As may beseem a monarch like himself.
   Myself have often heard him say and swear
124   That this his love was an eternal plant,
   Whereof the root was fixed in virtue's ground,
   The leaves and fruit maintained with beauty's sun,
127   Exempt from envy, but not from disdain,
   Unless the Lady Bonnë quit his pain.
KING LOUIS   *To Lady Bonne*
   Now, sister, let us hear your firm resolve.
LADY BONNE
130   Your grant, or your denial, shall be mine.
      To Warwick
   Yet I confess that often ere this day,
132   When I have heard your king's desert recounted,
   Mine ear hath tempted judgment to desire.
KING LOUIS   *To Warwick*
   Then, Warwick, thus – our sister shall be Edward's.
   And now, forthwith, shall articles be drawn

---

122 *beseem* befit   124 *eternal* i.e., heavenly   127–28 *Exempt . . . pain* i.e.,
Edward's love will be free from the effects of sharp criticism (*envy*) of Lady
Bonne (because of her coldness to his suit), but it will suffer from rejection
(*disdain*) unless she reward his passion for her (*quit his pain*)   130 *grant* con-
currence   132 *desert* merit

Touching the jointure that your king must make, 136
Which with her dowry shall be counterpoised. 137
   To Queen Margaret
Draw near, Queen Margaret, and be a witness
That Bonnë shall be wife to the English king.
   Queen Margaret, Prince Edward, and Oxford come
   forward.

PRINCE EDWARD
To Edward, but not to the English king. 140

QUEEN MARGARET
Deceitful Warwick – it was thy device
By this alliance to make void my suit!
Before thy coming Louis was Henry's friend.

KING LOUIS
And still is friend to him and Margaret.
But if your title to the crown be weak,
As may appear by Edward's good success,
Then 'tis but reason that I be released
From giving aid which late I promisèd. 148
Yet shall you have all kindness at my hand
That your estate requires and mine can yield. 150

WARWICK *To Queen Margaret*
Henry now lives in Scotland at his ease,
Where having nothing, nothing can he lose.
And as for you yourself, our quondam queen, 153
You have a father able to maintain you,
And better 'twere you troubled him than France.

QUEEN MARGARET
Peace, impudent and shameless Warwick, peace!
Proud setter up and puller down of kings!
I will not hence till, with my talk and tears,
Both full of truth, I make King Louis behold
Thy sly conveyance and thy lord's false love, 160

---

136 *jointure* marriage settlement **137** *counterpoised* matched **148** *late* recently **153** *quondam* former **160** *conveyance* trickery; **s.d.** *Post* dispatch rider

Post blowing a horn within.
For both of you are birds of selfsame feather.

KING LOUIS
Warwick, this is some post to us or thee.
Enter the Post.

POST *To Warwick*
My Lord Ambassador, these letters are for you,
Sent from your brother Marquis Montague;
To Louis
These from our king unto your majesty;
To Queen Margaret
And, madam, these for you, from whom I know not.
They all read their letters.

OXFORD *To Prince Edward*
I like it well that our fair queen and mistress
Smiles at her news, while Warwick frowns at his.

PRINCE EDWARD
Nay, mark how Louis stamps as he were nettled.
170 I hope all's for the best.

KING LOUIS
Warwick, what are thy news? And yours, fair queen?

QUEEN MARGARET
Mine, such as fill my heart with unhoped joys.

WARWICK
Mine, full of sorrow and heart's discontent.

KING LOUIS
What! Has your king married the Lady Grey?
175 And now to soothe your forgery and his,
Sends me a paper to persuade me patience?
Is this th' alliance that he seeks with France?
Dare he presume to scorn us in this manner?

QUEEN MARGARET
I told your majesty as much before –
180 This proveth Edward's love and Warwick's honesty.

WARWICK
King Louis, I here protest in sight of heaven

---

175 *soothe* smooth over; *forgery* deceit

And by the hope I have of heavenly bliss,
That I am clear from this misdeed of Edward's,
No more my king, for he dishonors me,
But most himself, if he could see his shame.
Did I forget that by the house of York
My father came untimely to his death?   187
Did I let pass th' abuse done to my niece?   188
Did I impale him with the regal crown?   189
Did I put Henry from his native right?   *190*
And am I guerdoned at the last with shame?   191
Shame on himself, for my desert is honor.
And to repair my honor, lost for him,
I here renounce him and return to Henry.
   To Queen Margaret
My noble queen, let former grudges pass,
And henceforth I am thy true servitor.   196
I will revenge his wrong to Lady Bonnë
And replant Henry in his former state.

QUEEN MARGARET
Warwick, these words have turned my hate to love,
And I forgive and quite forget old faults,   *200*
And joy that thou becom'st King Henry's friend.

WARWICK
So much his friend, ay, his unfeignèd friend,
That if King Louis vouchsafe to furnish us
With some few bands of chosen soldiers,
I'll undertake to land them on our coast
And force the tyrant from his seat by war.
'Tis not his new-made bride shall succor him.
And as for Clarence, as my letters tell me,
He's very likely now to fall from him   209

---

187 *My . . . death* (According to the chronicles, Warwick's father, the Salisbury of *2 Henry VI*, was captured by the Lancastrians at Wakefield and beheaded. Perhaps what Warwick means is that his father would not have died in the Yorkist cause had the Yorkists never laid claim to the throne.) 188 *Did . . . niece* (Holinshed reports that Edward "would have deflowered" Warwick's "daughter or his niece") 189 *impale him* encircle his brow 191 *guerdoned* rewarded 196 *servitor* servant 209 *fall from* desert

210   For matching more for wanton lust than honor,
       Or than for strength and safety of our country.
LADY BONNE   *To King Louis*
       Dear brother, how shall Bonnë be revenged,
       But by thy help to this distressèd queen?
QUEEN MARGARET   *To King Louis*
       Renownèd prince, how shall poor Henry live
       Unless thou rescue him from foul despair?
LADY BONNE   *To King Louis*
       My quarrel and this English queen's are one.
WARWICK
       And mine, fair Lady Bonnë, joins with yours.
KING LOUIS
       And mine with hers, and thine, and Margaret's.
       Therefore at last I firmly am resolved:
220   You shall have aid.
QUEEN MARGARET
       Let me give humble thanks for all at once.
KING LOUIS   *To the Post*
222   Then, England's messenger, return in post
       And tell false Edward, thy supposèd king,
224   That Louis of France is sending over masquers
       To revel it with him and his new bride.
226   Thou seest what's passed, go fear thy king withal.
LADY BONNE   *To the Post*
       Tell him, in hope he'll prove a widower shortly,
228   I'll wear the willow garland for his sake.
QUEEN MARGARET   *To the Post*
229   Tell him my mourning weeds are laid aside,
230   And I am ready to put armor on.
WARWICK   *To the Post*
       Tell him from me that he hath done me wrong,
       And therefore I'll uncrown him ere't be long.

---

210 *matching* marrying 222 *post* haste 224 *masquers* participants in the courtly dramatic performances, or revels, that were staged to celebrate aristocratic marriages (here meant ironically) 226 *fear* frighten; *withal* with it 228 *willow garland* (symbol of rejected love) 229 *weeds* garments

Giving money
There's thy reward – be gone.   *Exit Post.*
KING LOUIS
But, Warwick, thou and Oxford, with five thousand
    men,
Shall cross the seas and bid false Edward battle;
And, as occasion serves, this noble queen
And prince shall follow with a fresh supply.
Yet, ere thou go, but answer me one doubt:
What pledge have we of thy firm loyalty?
WARWICK
This shall assure my constant loyalty: 240
That if our queen and this young prince agree,
I'll join mine eldest daughter and my joy   242
To him forthwith in holy wedlock bands.
QUEEN MARGARET
Yes, I agree, and thank you for your motion.   244
    To Prince Edward
Son Edward, she is fair and virtuous,
Therefore delay not. Give thy hand to Warwick,
And with thy hand thy faith irrevocable
That only Warwick's daughter shall be thine.
PRINCE EDWARD
Yes, I accept her, for she well deserves it,
And here to pledge my vow I give my hand.   250
    He and Warwick clasp hands.
KING LOUIS
Why stay we now? These soldiers shall be levied,
And thou, Lord Bourbon, our high admiral,
Shall waft them over with our royal fleet.   253
I long till Edward fall by war's mischance
For mocking marriage with a dame of France.
                            Exeunt all but Warwick.

---

242 *eldest daughter* (Actually his younger daughter, Anne, as his elder daughter, Isabella, is to marry Clarence. In the chronicles, Isabella and Clarence are already married at this time.) 244 *motion* offer 253 *waft* transport by water

WARWICK
    I came from Edward as ambassador,
    But I return his sworn and mortal foe.
    Matter of marriage was the charge he gave me,
    But dreadful war shall answer his demand.
260   Had he none else to make a stale but me?
    Then none but I shall turn his jest to sorrow.
    I was the chief that raised him to the crown,
    And I'll be chief to bring him down again.
    Not that I pity Henry's misery,
    But seek revenge on Edward's mockery.   *Exit.*

*

∾ **IV.1** *Enter Richard Duke of Gloucester, George Duke*
    of Clarence, the Duke of Somerset, and the Marquis
    of Montague.

RICHARD DUKE OF GLOUCESTER
    Now tell me, brother Clarence, what think you
    Of this new marriage with the Lady Grey?
    Hath not our brother made a worthy choice?
GEORGE DUKE OF CLARENCE
    Alas, you know 'tis far from hence to France;
5   How could he stay till Warwick made return?
SOMERSET
    My lords, forbear this talk – here comes the king.
    Flourish. Enter King Edward, Elizabeth Lady Grey his
    Queen, the Earl of Pembroke, and the Lords Stafford
    and Hastings. Four stand on one side of the King,
    and four on the other.
RICHARD DUKE OF GLOUCESTER
    And his well-chosen bride.
GEORGE DUKE OF CLARENCE
8   I mind to tell him plainly what I think.

---

260 *stale* dupe
    IV.1 The palace, London   5 *stay* wait   8 *mind* intend

KING EDWARD
   Now, brother of Clarence, how like you our choice,
   That you stand pensive, as half malcontent?   10
GEORGE DUKE OF CLARENCE
   As well as Louis of France, or the Earl of Warwick,
   Which are so weak of courage and in judgment   12
   That they'll take no offense at our abuse.   13
KING EDWARD
   Suppose they take offense without a cause –
   They are but Louis and Warwick; I am Edward,
   Your king and Warwick's, and must have my will.   16
RICHARD DUKE OF GLOUCESTER
   And you shall have your will, because our king.
   Yet hasty marriage seldom proveth well.
KING EDWARD
   Yea, brother Richard, are you offended too?
RICHARD DUKE OF GLOUCESTER
   Not I, no – God forbid that I should wish them severed   20
   Whom God hath joined together. Ay, and 'twere pity
   To sunder them that yoke so well together.   22
KING EDWARD
   Setting your scorns and your mislike aside,   23
   Tell me some reason why the Lady Grey
   Should not become my wife and England's queen.
   And you too, Somerset and Montague,
   Speak freely what you think.
GEORGE DUKE OF CLARENCE
   Then this is my opinion: that King Louis
   Becomes your enemy for mocking him
   About the marriage of the Lady Bonnë.   30
RICHARD DUKE OF GLOUCESTER
   And Warwick, doing what you gave in charge,
   Is now dishonorèd by this new marriage.

---

10 *malcontent* disgusted with the world   12 *Which* who   13 *abuse* insult
16 *will* (1) way, (2) sexual desire satisfied   22 *that yoke* who are joined (in
marriage)   23 *mislike* displeasure

KING EDWARD

  What if both Louis and Warwick be appeased

34 By such invention as I can devise?

MONTAGUE

  Yet, to have joined with France in such alliance

  Would more have strengthened this our common-
    wealth

  'Gainst foreign storms than any home-bred marriage.

HASTINGS

  Why, knows not Montague that of itself

  England is safe, if true within itself?

MONTAGUE

40 But the safer when 'tis backed with France.

HASTINGS

  'Tis better using France than trusting France.

  Let us be backed with God and with the seas

  Which he hath giv'n for fence impregnable,

44 And with their helps only defend ourselves.

  In them and in ourselves our safety lies.

GEORGE DUKE OF CLARENCE

  For this one speech Lord Hastings well deserves

47 To have the heir of the Lord Hungerford.

KING EDWARD

  Ay, what of that? It was my will and grant –

  And for this once my will shall stand for law.

RICHARD DUKE OF GLOUCESTER

50 And yet, methinks, your grace hath not done well

  To give the heir and daughter of Lord Scales

52 Unto the brother of your loving bride.

  She better would have fitted me or Clarence,

54 But in your bride you bury brotherhood.

GEORGE DUKE OF CLARENCE

  Or else you would not have bestowed the heir

---

34 *invention* plan   44 *only* alone   47 *heir ... Hungerford* i.e., a wealthy
heiress (George's point is that Lady Grey's upstart relatives, such as Hastings,
are inappropriately being matched with wealthy partners)   52 *brother ...
bride* i.e., Lord Rivers   54 *But in* because of; *bury* forget

Of the Lord Bonville on your new wife's son,   56
And leave your brothers to go speed elsewhere.   57

KING EDWARD
Alas, poor Clarence, is it for a wife
That thou art malcontent? I will provide thee.

GEORGE DUKE OF CLARENCE
In choosing for yourself you showed your judgment,   60
Which being shallow, you shall give me leave
To play the broker in mine own behalf,   62
And to that end I shortly mind to leave you.

KING EDWARD
Leave me, or tarry. Edward will be king,
And not be tied unto his brother's will.

QUEEN ELIZABETH
My lords, before it pleased his majesty
To raise my state to title of a queen,
Do me but right, and you must all confess
That I was not ignoble of descent –
And meaner than myself have had like fortune.   70
But as this title honors me and mine,
So your dislikes, to whom I would be pleasing,   72
Doth cloud my joys with danger and with sorrow.   73

KING EDWARD
My love, forbear to fawn upon their frowns.   74
What danger or what sorrow can befall thee
So long as Edward is thy constant friend,
And their true sovereign, whom they must obey?
Nay, whom they shall obey, and love thee too –
Unless they seek for hatred at my hands,
Which if they do, yet will I keep thee safe,   80
And they shall feel the vengeance of my wrath.

RICHARD DUKE OF GLOUCESTER   *Aside*
I hear, yet say not much, but think the more.

---

56 *son* i.e., Sir Thomas Grey, Marquis of Dorset   57 *go speed* prosper (for
themselves)   62 *broker* agent   70 *meaner* persons of lower social rank; *like
fortune* (Not true: Elizabeth Woodville was the first commoner to become a
queen of England.)   72 *dislikes* disapproval   73 *danger* apprehension   74
forbear . . . frowns pay no attention to their disapproval

Enter the Post from France.

KING EDWARD
Now, messenger, what letters or what news from France?

POST
My sovereign liege, no letters and few words,
But such as I, without your special pardon,
Dare not relate.

KING EDWARD
87   Go to, we pardon thee. Therefore, in brief,
88   Tell me their words as near as thou canst guess them.
What answer makes King Louis unto our letters?

POST
90   At my depart these were his very words:
"Go tell false Edward, thy supposèd king,
That Louis of France is sending over masquers
To revel it with him and his new bride."

KING EDWARD
94   Is Louis so brave? Belike he thinks me Henry.
But what said Lady Bonnë to my marriage?

POST
These were her words, uttered with mild disdain:
"Tell him, in hope he'll prove a widower shortly,
I'll wear the willow garland for his sake."

KING EDWARD
I blame not her, she could say little less;
100   She had the wrong. But what said Henry's queen?
101   For I have heard that she was there in place.

POST
"Tell him," quoth she, "my mourning weeds are done,
And I am ready to put armor on."

KING EDWARD
Belike she minds to play the Amazon.
But what said Warwick to these injuries?

POST
He, more incensed against your majesty

___

87 *Go to* all right, don't worry   88 *guess* approximate   90 *depart* departure
94 *Belike* perhaps   101 *in place* present

Than all the rest, discharged me with these words:
"Tell him from me that he hath done me wrong,
And therefore I'll uncrown him ere't be long."

KING EDWARD
Ha! Durst the traitor breathe out so proud words?   110
Well, I will arm me, being thus forewarned.
They shall have wars and pay for their presumption.
But say, is Warwick friends with Margaret?

POST
Ay, gracious sovereign, they are so linked in friendship
That young Prince Edward marries Warwick's daughter.

GEORGE DUKE OF CLARENCE
Belike the elder; Clarence will have the younger.   116
Now, brother king, farewell, and sit you fast,
For I will hence to Warwick's other daughter,
That, though I want a kingdom, yet in marriage   119
I may not prove inferior to yourself.   120
You that love me and Warwick, follow me.
                     Exit Clarence, and Somerset follows.

RICHARD DUKE OF GLOUCESTER
Not I – *(Aside)* my thoughts aim at a further matter.
I stay not for the love of Edward, but the crown.

KING EDWARD
Clarence and Somerset both gone to Warwick?
Yet am I armed against the worst can happen,
And haste is needful in this desp'rate case.
Pembroke and Stafford, you in our behalf
Go levy men and make prepare for war.   128
They are already, or quickly will be, landed.
Myself in person will straight follow you.   130
                    Exeunt Pembroke and Stafford.
But ere I go, Hastings and Montague,
Resolve my doubt. You twain, of all the rest,
Are near'st to Warwick by blood and by alliance.
Tell me if you love Warwick more than me.

---

116 *Belike . . . younger* (see the note to III.3.242)   119 *want* lack   128 *prepare* preparation

If it be so, then both depart to him —
136   I rather wish you foes than hollow friends.
But if you mind to hold your true obedience,
Give me assurance with some friendly vow
139   That I may never have you in suspect.
MONTAGUE
140   So God help Montague as he proves true.
HASTINGS
And Hastings as he favors Edward's cause.
KING EDWARD
Now, brother Richard, will you stand by us?
RICHARD DUKE OF GLOUCESTER
Ay, in despite of all that shall withstand you.
KING EDWARD
Why, so. Then am I sure of victory.
Now, therefore, let us hence and lose no hour
146   Till we meet Warwick with his foreign power.   *Exeunt.*

*

❧ **IV.2** *Enter the Earls of Warwick and Oxford
in England, with French Soldiers.*

WARWICK
Trust me, my lord, all hitherto goes well.
The common sort by numbers swarm to us.
Enter the Dukes of Clarence and Somerset.
But see where Somerset and Clarence comes.
Speak suddenly, my lords, are we all friends?
GEORGE DUKE OF CLARENCE
Fear not that, my lord.
WARWICK
Then, gentle Clarence, welcome unto Warwick —
And welcome, Somerset. I hold it cowardice
To rest mistrustful where a noble heart

---

136 *hollow* empty (i.e., untrustworthy)   **139** *suspect* suspicion   **146** *power* army
IV.2 Fields near Warwick   **1** *hitherto* so far

Hath pawned an open hand in sign of love, 9
Else might I think that Clarence, Edward's brother, 10
Were but a feignèd friend to our proceedings.
But come, sweet Clarence, my daughter shall be thine.
And now what rests but, in night's coverture, 13
Thy brother being carelessly encamped,
His soldiers lurking in the towns about, 15
And but attended by a simple guard,
We may surprise and take him at our pleasure?
Our scouts have found the adventure very easy;
That, as Ulysses and stout Diomed 19
With sleight and manhood stole to Rhesus' tents 20
And brought from thence the Thracian fatal steeds,
So we, well covered with the night's black mantle,
At unawares may beat down Edward's guard 23
And seize himself – I say not "slaughter him,"
For I intend but only to surprise him. 25
You that will follow me to this attempt,
Applaud the name of Henry with your leader.
    They all cry "Henry!"
Why, then, let's on our way in silent sort, 28
For Warwick and his friends, God and Saint George!
                                                    Exeunt.

*

<hr>

9 *pawned* pledged   13 *rests* remains; *in night's coverture* under cover of night
15 *lurking* idling   19–21 *That . . . steeds* (The oracle predicted that Troy
would not fall if the horses of Rhesus, king of Thrace, grazed on the Trojan
plain. To prevent their doing so, Ulysses and Diomedes captured them on a
night raid.)   20 *sleight* stealth; *manhood* manly actions, bravery   23 *At unawares* suddenly   25 *surprise* capture   28 *sort* manner

⮂ **IV.3** *Enter three Watchmen, to guard King Edward's tent.*

FIRST WATCHMAN

1   Come on, my masters, each man take his stand.
2   The king by this is set him down to sleep.

SECOND WATCHMAN

What, will he not to bed?

FIRST WATCHMAN

Why, no – for he hath made a solemn vow
Never to lie and take his natural rest
6   Till Warwick or himself be quite suppressed.

SECOND WATCHMAN

Tomorrow then belike shall be the day,
If Warwick be so near as men report.

THIRD WATCHMAN

But say, I pray, what nobleman is that
10   That with the king here resteth in his tent?

FIRST WATCHMAN

'Tis the Lord Hastings, the king's chiefest friend.

THIRD WATCHMAN

O, is it so? But why commands the king
That his chief followers lodge in towns about him,
14   While he himself keeps in the cold field?

SECOND WATCHMAN

'Tis the more honor, because more dangerous.

THIRD WATCHMAN

16   Ay, but give me worship and quietness –
I like it better than a dangerous honor.
18   If Warwick knew in what estate he stands,
19   'Tis to be doubted he would waken him.

FIRST WATCHMAN

20   Unless our halberds did shut up his passage.

IV.3 King Edward's camp, near Warwick   1 *stand* post   2 *this* i.e., this time;
set him down settled in a chair   6 *suppressed* defeated   14 *keeps* lodges   16
worship a place of dignity   18 *estate* condition; *he* King Edward   19
doubted feared   20 *halberds* axlike weapons on long staves; *shut up* bar

SECOND WATCHMAN
    Ay, wherefore else guard we his royal tent
    But to defend his person from night foes?
        *Enter silently the Earl of Warwick, George Duke of
        Clarence, the Earl of Oxford, and the Duke of
        Somerset, with French Soldiers.*

WARWICK
    This is his tent – and see where stand his guard.
    Courage, my masters – honor now or never!
    But follow me, and Edward shall be ours.
FIRST WATCHMAN   Who goes there?
SECOND WATCHMAN   Stay or thou diest.
        *Warwick and the rest all cry "Warwick, Warwick!"
        and set upon the Guard, who fly, crying "Arm, arm!"
        Warwick and the rest follow them.*

*

✖ **IV.4** *With the Drummer playing and the Trumpeter
    sounding, enter the Earl of Warwick, the Duke of
    Somerset, and the rest, bringing King Edward out
    in his gown, sitting in a chair. Richard Duke of
    Gloucester and Lord Hastings flee over the stage.*

SOMERSET
    What are they that fly there?
WARWICK
    Richard and Hastings – let them go. Here is the duke.
KING EDWARD
    "The duke"! Why, Warwick, when we parted,
    Thou calledst me king.   4
WARWICK   Ay, but the case is altered.
    When you disgraced me in my embassade,   5
    Then I degraded you from being king,
    And come now to create you Duke of York.
    Alas, how should you govern any kingdom

IV.4 King Edward's camp **4** *the case is altered* things have changed (prover-
bial) **5** *embassade* diplomatic mission

That know not how to use ambassadors,
10 Nor how to be contented with one wife,
Nor how to use your brothers brotherly,
Nor how to study for the people's welfare,
13 Nor how to shroud yourself from enemies?

KING EDWARD *Seeing George*
Yea, brother of Clarence, art thou here too?
15 Nay, then, I see that Edward needs must down.
Yet, Warwick, in despite of all mischance,
17 Of thee thyself and all thy complices,
Edward will always bear himself as king.
19 Though fortune's malice overthrow my state,
20 My mind exceeds the compass of her wheel.

WARWICK
21 Then, for his mind, be Edward England's king.
Warwick takes off Edward's crown.
But Henry now shall wear the English crown,
And be true king indeed, thou but the shadow.
My Lord of Somerset, at my request,
See that, forthwith, Duke Edward be conveyed
26 Unto my brother, Archbishop of York.
When I have fought with Pembroke and his fellows,
I'll follow you, and tell what answer
Louis and the Lady Bonnë send to him.
30 Now for a while farewell, good Duke of York.
They begin to lead Edward out forcibly.

KING EDWARD
31 What fates impose, that men must needs abide.
32 It boots not to resist both wind and tide.
                          Exeunt some with Edward.

OXFORD
What now remains, my lords, for us to do

---

13 *shroud* conceal, protect 15 *needs must down* must necessarily be put down 17 *complices* accomplices 19 *state* sovereignty 20 *compass* circumference 21 *for his* in Edward's 26 *Archbishop of York* i.e., George Neville 31 *abide* endure 32 *boots not* is no use

But march to London with our soldiers?
WARWICK
   Ay, that's the first thing that we have to do –
   To free King Henry from imprisonment
   And see him seated in the regal throne.   *Exeunt.*

                              *

∾ **IV.5** *Enter Earl Rivers and his sister Queen Elizabeth.*

RIVERS
   Madam, what makes you in this sudden change?   1
QUEEN ELIZABETH
   Why, brother Rivers, are you yet to learn
   What late misfortune is befall'n King Edward?
RIVERS
   What? Loss of some pitched battle against Warwick?
QUEEN ELIZABETH
   No, but the loss of his own royal person.
RIVERS
   Then is my sovereign slain?
QUEEN ELIZABETH
   Ay, almost slain – for he is taken prisoner,
   Either betrayed by falsehood of his guard
   Or by his foe surprised at unawares,
   And, as I further have to understand,   10
   Is new committed to the Bishop of York,   11
   Fell Warwick's brother, and by that our foe.   12
RIVERS
   These news, I must confess, are full of grief.
   Yet, gracious madam, bear it as you may.
   Warwick may lose, that now hath won the day.
QUEEN ELIZABETH
   Till then fair hope must hinder life's decay,

IV.5 The palace, London 1 *what ... change?* why have you suddenly
changed your mind 11 *new* recently; *Bishop* i.e., archbishop 12 *Fell* cruel;
by that i.e., because of that relationship

17   And I the rather wean me from despair
       For love of Edward's offspring in my womb.
19   This is it that makes me bridle passion
20   And bear with mildness my misfortune's cross.
       Ay, ay, for this I draw in many a tear
22   And stop the rising of bloodsucking sighs,
23   Lest with my sighs or tears I blast or drown
       King Edward's fruit, true heir to th' English crown.

RIVERS
25   But, madam, where is Warwick then become?

QUEEN ELIZABETH
       I am informèd that he comes towards London
       To set the crown once more on Henry's head.
       Guess thou the rest – King Edward's friends must down.
29   But to prevent the tyrant's violence –
30   For trust not him that hath once broken faith –
31   I'll hence forthwith unto the sanctuary,
       To save at least the heir of Edward's right.
       There shall I rest secure from force and fraud.
       Come, therefore, let us fly while we may fly.
       If Warwick take us, we are sure to die.   *Exeunt.*

               *

∾ **IV.6** *Enter Richard Duke of Gloucester, Lord
     Hastings, and Sir William Stanley, with Soldiers.*

RICHARD DUKE OF GLOUCESTER
       Now my Lord Hastings and Sir William Stanley,
       Leave off to wonder why I drew you hither
3   Into this chiefest thicket of the park.
       Thus stands the case: you know our king, my brother,
       Is prisoner to the bishop here, at whose hands

---

17 *I the rather* I am the more obliged to   19 *bridle* control   22 *bloodsucking sighs* (sighing was supposed to waste the heart's blood, which explains why *hope* can *hinder life's decay* in l. 16)   23 *blast* wither   25 *become* gone   29 *prevent* forestall   31 *sanctuary* (where I will be immune from arrest)
    IV.6 The Archbishop of York's park, or hunting ground, near Warwick 3 *chiefest* largest; *park* hunting ground

He hath good usage and great liberty,
And, often but attended with weak guard,
Comes hunting this way to disport himself.   8
I have advertised him by secret means   9
That if about this hour he make this way   10
Under the color of his usual game,   11
He shall here find his friends with horse and men
To set him free from his captivity.
   Enter King Edward and a Huntsman with him.

HUNTSMAN
   This way, my lord – for this way lies the game.
KING EDWARD
   Nay, this way, man – see where the huntsmen stand.
   Now, brother of Gloucester, Lord Hastings, and the
      rest,
   Stand you thus close to steal the bishop's deer?   17
RICHARD DUKE OF GLOUCESTER
   Brother, the time and case requireth haste.
   Your horse stands ready at the park corner.
KING EDWARD
   But whither shall we then?   20
HASTINGS
   To Lynn, my lord,   21
   And shipped from thence to Flanders.
RICHARD DUKE OF GLOUCESTER   *Aside*
   Well guessed, believe me – for that was my meaning.
KING EDWARD
   Stanley, I will requite thy forwardness.   24
RICHARD DUKE OF GLOUCESTER
   But wherefore stay we? 'Tis no time to talk.
KING EDWARD
   Huntsman, what sayst thou? Wilt thou go along?
HUNTSMAN
   Better do so than tarry and be hanged.

---

8 *disport* amuse   9 *advertised* notified   11 *color* pretext; *game* hunting (i.e.,
as though he were merely hunting)   17 *close* hidden   21 *Lynn* i.e., King's
Lynn, on the Norfolk coast   24 *requite* reward; *forwardness* zeal

RICHARD DUKE OF GLOUCESTER
  Come then, away – let's have no more ado.
KING EDWARD
  Bishop, farewell – shield thee from Warwick's frown,
30 And pray that I may repossess the crown.   *Exeunt.*

                    *

∾ **IV.7** *Flourish. Enter the Earl of Warwick and George*
    Duke of Clarence with the crown. Then enter King
    Henry, the Earl of Oxford, the Duke of Somerset with
    young Henry Earl of Richmond, the Marquis of
    Montague, and the Lieutenant of the Tower.

KING HENRY
  Master Lieutenant, now that God and friends
  Have shaken Edward from the regal seat
  And turned my captive state to liberty,
  My fear to hope, my sorrows unto joys,
5 At our enlargement what are thy due fees?
LIEUTENANT
6 Subjects may challenge nothing of their sovereigns –
  But if an humble prayer may prevail,
  I then crave pardon of your majesty.
KING HENRY
  For what, lieutenant? For well using me?
10 Nay, be thou sure I'll well requite thy kindness,
  For that it made my prisonment a pleasure –
  Ay, such a pleasure as encagèd birds
  Conceive when, after many moody thoughts,
  At last by notes of household harmony
  They quite forget their loss of liberty.
  But, Warwick, after God, thou sett'st me free,
  And chiefly therefore I thank God and thee.
  He was the author, thou the instrument.

IV.7 The Tower, London **s.d.** *Lieutenant* deputy warden **5** *enlargement* re-
lease; *fees* (due because prisoners who could afford it were charged for special
quarters and food) **6** *challenge* demand

Therefore, that I may conquer fortune's spite
By living low, where fortune cannot hurt me,   20
And that the people of this blessèd land
May not be punished with my thwarting stars,   22
Warwick, although my head still wear the crown,
I here resign my government to thee,
For thou art fortunate in all thy deeds.

WARWICK
Your grace hath still been famed for virtuous,   26
And now may seem as wise as virtuous
By spying and avoiding fortune's malice,
For few men rightly temper with the stars.   29
Yet in this one thing let me blame your grace: 30
For choosing me when Clarence is in place.   31

GEORGE DUKE OF CLARENCE
No, Warwick, thou art worthy of the sway,   32
To whom the heav'ns in thy nativity   33
Adjudged an olive branch and laurel crown,   34
As likely to be blest in peace and war.
And therefore I yield thee my free consent.

WARWICK
And I choose Clarence only for Protector.   37

KING HENRY
Warwick and Clarence, give me both your hands.
Now join your hands, and with your hands your hearts,
That no dissension hinder government.   40
I make you both Protectors of this land,
While I myself will lead a private life
And in devotion spend my latter days,
To sin's rebuke and my creator's praise.

---

20 *low* humbly   **22** *thwarting stars* (1) bad luck, (2) stars (instruments of
fortune) whose influence impedes happiness and success   **26** *still* always
29 *temper . . . stars* i.e., come to terms with their fate   **31** *in place* here   **32**
sway rule   **33** *nativity* birth (an allusion to astrological determinism)   **34**
olive branch (a symbol of peace); *laurel crown* (a symbol of victory)   **37** *only*
alone; *Protector* i.e., a kind of deputy king, who ruled during the minority or
incapacity of the monarch (Humphrey, Duke of Gloucester, held this posi-
tion in *2 Henry VI*)

WARWICK
   What answers Clarence to his sovereign's will?
GEORGE DUKE OF CLARENCE
   That he consents, if Warwick yield consent,
   For on thy fortune I repose myself.
WARWICK
   Why, then, though loath, yet must I be content.
   We'll yoke together, like a double shadow
50   To Henry's body, and supply his place –
   I mean in bearing weight of government –
   While he enjoys the honor and his ease.
   And, Clarence, now then it is more than needful
   Forthwith that Edward be pronounced a traitor,
   And all his lands and goods be confiscate.
GEORGE DUKE OF CLARENCE
   What else? And that succession be determined.
WARWICK
57   Ay, therein Clarence shall not want his part.
KING HENRY
   But with the first of all your chief affairs,
   Let me entreat – for I command no more –
60   That Margaret your queen and my son Edward
   Be sent for, to return from France with speed.
   For, till I see them here, by doubtful fear
   My joy of liberty is half eclipsed.
GEORGE DUKE OF CLARENCE
   It shall be done, my sovereign, with all speed.
KING HENRY
   My Lord of Somerset, what youth is that
   Of whom you seem to have so tender care?
SOMERSET
67   My liege, it is young Henry, Earl of Richmond.

---

50 *supply* take   57 *want* lack; *his part* (should the Lancastrian claim be dismissed and Edward proclaimed a traitor, Clarence would be next in line to the throne)   67 *Henry* (the future Henry VII; at his accession to the throne the Wars of the Roses finally ceased)

KING HENRY
  Come hither, England's hope.
      King Henry lays his hand on Richmond's head.
                          If secret powers
  Suggest but truth to my divining thoughts,   69
  This pretty lad will prove our country's bliss.   70
  His looks are full of peaceful majesty,
  His head by nature framed to wear a crown,
  His hand to wield a scepter, and himself
  Likely in time to bless a regal throne.
  Make much of him, my lords, for this is he
  Must help you more than you are hurt by me.
      Enter a Post.
WARWICK
  What news, my friend?
POST
  That Edward is escapèd from your brother
  And fled, as he hears since, to Burgundy.   79
WARWICK
  Unsavory news – but how made he escape?   80
POST
  He was conveyed by Richard Duke of Gloucester   81
  And the Lord Hastings, who attended him   82
  In secret ambush on the forest side
  And from the bishop's huntsmen rescued him –
  For hunting was his daily exercise.
WARWICK
  My brother was too careless of his charge.
      To King Henry
  But let us hence, my sovereign, to provide
  A salve for any sore that may betide.   88
          Exeunt all but Somerset, Richmond, and Oxford.
SOMERSET   *To Oxford*
  My lord, I like not of this flight of Edward's,

---

69 *divining* prophesying   **79** *he* i.e., your brother, the Archbishop of York
81 *conveyed* secretly carried away   **82** *attended* waited for   **88** *betide* develop

90 For doubtless Burgundy will yield him help,
And we shall have more wars before't be long.
As Henry's late presaging prophecy
Did glad my heart with hope of this young Richmond,
So doth my heart misgive me, in these conflicts,
What may befall him, to his harm and ours.
Therefore, Lord Oxford, to prevent the worst,
Forthwith we'll send him hence to Brittany,
Till storms be past of civil enmity.

OXFORD
Ay, for if Edward repossess the crown,
100 'Tis like that Richmond with the rest shall down.

SOMERSET
It shall be so – he shall to Brittany.
Come, therefore, let's about it speedily.   *Exeunt.*

*

∾ **IV.8** *Flourish. Enter King Edward, Richard Duke
of Gloucester, and Lord Hastings, with a troop of
Hollanders.*

KING EDWARD
Now, brother Richard, Lord Hastings, and the rest,
Yet thus far fortune maketh us amends,
And says that once more I shall interchange
4 My wanèd state for Henry's regal crown.
Well have we passed and now repassed the seas
And brought desirèd help from Burgundy.
What then remains, we being thus arrived
8 From Ravenspurgh haven before the gates of York,
But that we enter, as into our dukedom?
Hastings knocks at the gates of York.

RICHARD DUKE OF GLOUCESTER
10 The gates made fast? Brother, I like not this.

---

100 *down* fall
IV.8 Outside the walls of York   **4** *wanèd* faded, declined   **8** *Ravenspurgh*
(on the Yorkshire coast, at the mouth of the River Humber)

For many men that stumble at the threshold   11
Are well foretold that danger lurks within.
KING EDWARD
Tush, man, abodements must not now affright us.   13
By fair or foul means we must enter in,
For hither will our friends repair to us.
HASTINGS
My liege, I'll knock once more to summon them.
    He knocks.
    Enter, on the walls, the Mayor and Aldermen of York.
MAYOR
My lords, we were forewarnèd of your coming,
And shut the gates for safety of ourselves –
For now we owe allegiance unto Henry.
KING EDWARD
But, Master Mayor, if Henry be your king,   20
Yet Edward at the least is Duke of York.
MAYOR
True, my good lord, I know you for no less.
KING EDWARD
Why, and I challenge nothing but my dukedom,   23
As being well content with that alone.
RICHARD DUKE OF GLOUCESTER   *Aside*
But when the fox hath once got in his nose,
He'll soon find means to make the body follow.
HASTINGS
Why, Master Mayor, why stand you in a doubt?
Open the gates – we are King Henry's friends.
MAYOR
Ay, say you so? The gates shall then be opened.
    They descend.
RICHARD DUKE OF GLOUCESTER
A wise stout captain, and soon persuaded.   30
HASTINGS
The good old man would fain that all were well,   31

---

11 *stumble . . . threshold* (a sign of bad luck)   13 *abodements* omens   23
challenge claim   30 *stout* valiant   31 *would fain* desires

32   So 'twere not long of him; but being entered,
      I doubt not, I, but we shall soon persuade
      Both him and all his brothers unto reason.
        Enter below the Mayor and two Aldermen.
      KING EDWARD
      So, Master Mayor, these gates must not be shut
      But in the night or in the time of war.
      What – fear not, man, but yield me up the keys,
        King Edward takes some keys from the Mayor.
      For Edward will defend the town and thee,
39   And all those friends that deign to follow me.
        March. Enter Sir John Montgomery, with a Drummer
        and Soldiers.
      RICHARD DUKE OF GLOUCESTER
40   Brother, this is Sir John Montgomery,
      Our trusty friend, unless I be deceived.
      KING EDWARD
      Welcome, Sir John – but why come you in arms?
      MONTGOMERY
      To help King Edward in his time of storm,
      As every loyal subject ought to do.
      KING EDWARD
      Thanks, good Montgomery, but we now forget
      Our title to the crown, and only claim
      Our dukedom till God please to send the rest.
      MONTGOMERY
      Then fare you well, for I will hence again.
      I came to serve a king and not a duke.
50   Drummer, strike up, and let us march away.
        The Drummer begins to sound a march.
      KING EDWARD
      Nay, stay, Sir John, a while, and we'll debate

---

32 *So . . . him* as long as he bears no responsibility   39 *deign* are willing   40
Sir John Montgomery (called Sir Thomas in the chronicles, which report that
he met Edward at Nottingham after the securing of the city of York)   50 s.d.
begins . . . march commences beating a march

By what safe means the crown may be recovered.
MONTGOMERY
  What talk you of debating? In few words,
  If you'll not here proclaim yourself our king
  I'll leave you to your fortune and be gone
  To keep them back that come to succor you.
  Why shall we fight, if you pretend no title?   57
RICHARD DUKE OF GLOUCESTER   *To King Edward*
  Why, brother, wherefore stand you on nice points?   58
KING EDWARD
  When we grow stronger, then we'll make our claim.
  Till then 'tis wisdom to conceal our meaning.   60
HASTINGS
  Away with scrupulous wit! Now arms must rule.   61
RICHARD DUKE OF GLOUCESTER
  And fearless minds climb soonest unto crowns.
  Brother, we will proclaim you out of hand,   63
  The bruit thereof will bring you many friends.   64
KING EDWARD
  Then be it as you will, for 'tis my right,
  And Henry but usurps the diadem.
MONTGOMERY
  Ay, now my sovereign speaketh like himself,
  And now will I be Edward's champion.   68
HASTINGS
  Sound trumpet, Edward shall be here proclaimed.
    To Montgomery
  Come, fellow soldier, make thou proclamation.   70
    Flourish.
MONTGOMERY   Edward the Fourth, by the grace of God
  King of England and France, and Lord of Ireland –
  And whosoe'er gainsays King Edward's right,   73
  By this I challenge him to single fight.   74
    He throws down his gauntlet.

---

57 *pretend* claim   58 *stand* dwell; *nice points* minor details   61 *wit* reasoning   63 *out of hand* immediately   64 *bruit* news   68 *champion* defender   73 *gainsays* denies   74 s.d. *gauntlet* glove (a challenge to a duel)

ALL   Long live Edward the Fourth!

KING EDWARD

Thanks, brave Montgomery, and thanks unto you all.

77   If fortune serve me I'll requite this kindness.

Now, for this night, let's harbor here in York;

79   And when the morning sun shall raise his car

80   Above the border of this horizon,

We'll forward towards Warwick and his mates.

82   For well I wot that Henry is no soldier.

83   Ah, froward Clarence, how evil it beseems thee

To flatter Henry and forsake thy brother!

Yet, as we may, we'll meet both thee and Warwick.

Come on, brave soldiers – doubt not of the day

And, that once gotten, doubt not of large pay. *Exeunt.*

*

∾ **IV.9** *Flourish. Enter King Henry, the Earl of*
Warwick, the Marquis of Montague, George
Duke of Clarence, and the Earl of Oxford.

WARWICK

1   What counsel, lords? Edward from Belgia,

2   With hasty Germans and blunt Hollanders,

Hath passed in safety through the narrow seas,

4   And with his troops doth march amain to London,

And many giddy people flock to him.

KING HENRY

Let's levy men and beat him back again.

GEORGE DUKE OF CLARENCE

A little fire is quickly trodden out,

8   Which, being suffered, rivers cannot quench.

WARWICK

In Warwickshire I have true-hearted friends,

10   Not mutinous in peace, yet bold in war.

---

77 *requite* repay 79 *car* chariot 82 *wot* know 83 *froward* perverse
    IV.9 The Bishop of London's palace 1 *Belgia* the Netherlands 2 *hasty*
rash, quick-tempered; *blunt* merciless 4 *amain* speedily 8 *suffered* tolerated

Those will I muster up. And thou, son Clarence,   11
Shalt stir in Suffolk, Norfolk, and in Kent,
The knights and gentlemen to come with thee.
Thou, brother Montague, in Buckingham,
Northampton, and in Leicestershire shalt find
Men well inclined to hear what thou command'st.
And thou, brave Oxford, wondrous well beloved
In Oxfordshire, shalt muster up thy friends.
My sovereign, with the loving citizens,
Like to his island girt in with the ocean,   20
Or modest Dian circled with her nymphs,   21
Shall rest in London till we come to him.
Fair lords, take leave and stand not to reply.
Farewell, my sovereign.

KING HENRY
Farewell, my Hector, and my Troy's true hope.   25

GEORGE DUKE OF CLARENCE
In sign of truth, I kiss your highness' hand.
    He kisses King Henry's hand.

KING HENRY
Well-minded Clarence, be thou fortunate.

MONTAGUE
Comfort, my lord, and so I take my leave.
    He kisses King Henry's hand.

OXFORD
And thus I seal my truth and bid adieu.   29
    He kisses King Henry's hand.

KING HENRY
Sweet Oxford, and my loving Montague,   30
And all at once, once more a happy farewell.   *Exit.*   31

---

11 *son* i.e., son-in-law   21 *Dian* Diana (in Roman mythology the goddess of the moon, hunting, and chastity, with whom Queen Elizabeth was often associated)   25 *Hector* greatest warrior of Troy; *my Troy's* (because London [New Troy] was supposedly founded by Brutus, legendary grandson of the Trojan hero Aeneas)   29 *seal my truth* affirm my loyalty   31 *at once* together

WARWICK

32   Farewell, sweet lords – let's meet at Coventry.

Exeunt severally.

*

∾ **IV.10** *Enter King Henry and the Duke of Exeter.*

KING HENRY
    Here at the palace will I rest a while.
    Cousin of Exeter, what thinks your lordship?
    Methinks the power that Edward hath in field
    Should not be able to encounter mine.

EXETER

5   The doubt is that he will seduce the rest.

KING HENRY

6   That's not my fear. My meed hath got me fame.
    I have not stopped mine ears to their demands,

8   Nor posted off their suits with slow delays.
    My pity hath been balm to heal their wounds,

10   My mildness hath allayed their swelling griefs,
    My mercy dried their water-flowing tears.
    I have not been desirous of their wealth,

13   Nor much oppressed them with great subsidies,

14   Nor forward of revenge, though they much erred.
    Then why should they love Edward more than me?

16   No, Exeter, these graces challenge grace;
    And when the lion fawns upon the lamb,
    The lamb will never cease to follow him.

    Shout within: "A Lancaster!" "A York!"

EXETER
    Hark, hark, my lord – what shouts are these?

    Enter King Edward and Richard Duke of Gloucester,
    with Soldiers.

---

32 s.d. *severally* separately
    IV.10 The bishop's palace **5** *doubt* fear **6** *meed* merit, generosity; *got* won
8 *posted off* (1) treated lightly, (2) postponed **13** *subsidies* taxes **14** *forward of* eager for **16** *challenge grace* claim favor

KING EDWARD
  Seize on the shamefaced Henry – bear him hence,   20
  And once again proclaim us King of England.
  You are the fount that makes small brooks to flow.
  Now stops thy spring – my sea shall suck them dry,
  And swell so much the higher by their ebb.
  Hence with him to the Tower – let him not speak.
        Exeunt some with King Henry and Exeter.
  And lords, towards Coventry bend we our course,
  Where peremptory Warwick now remains.   27
  The sun shines hot, and, if we use delay,   28
  Cold biting winter mars our hoped-for hay.
RICHARD DUKE OF GLOUCESTER
  Away betimes, before his forces join,   30
  And take the great-grown traitor unawares.
  Brave warriors, march amain towards Coventry.
                      Exeunt.

*

∾ **V.1** *Enter the Earl of Warwick, the Mayor of*
    Coventry, two Messengers, and others upon
    the walls.

WARWICK
  Where is the post that came from valiant Oxford?
    The First Messenger steps forward.
  How far hence is thy lord, mine honest fellow?
FIRST MESSENGER
  By this at Dunsmore, marching hitherward.   3
WARWICK
  How far off is our brother Montague?
  Where is the post that came from Montague?
    The Second Messenger steps forward.

---

20 *shamefaced* timid 27 *peremptory* overbearing 28–29 *The sun . . . hay*
we should seize this opportunity (i.e., we should make hay while the sun
shines) 30 *betimes* at once
  V.1 Before the walls of Coventry 3 *this* this time; *Dunsmore* Dunsmore
Heath, between Coventry and Daventry

SECOND MESSENGER

6 By this at Da'ntry, with a puissant troop.
  Enter Somerville to them, above.

WARWICK

 Say, Somerville – what says my loving son?
 And, by thy guess, how nigh is Clarence now?

SOMERVILLE

9 At Southam I did leave him with his forces,
10 And do expect him here some two hours hence.
  A march afar off.

WARWICK

 Then Clarence is at hand – I hear his drum.

SOMERVILLE

12 It is not his, my lord. Here Southam lies.
 The drum your honor hears marcheth from Warwick.

WARWICK

14 Who should that be? Belike, unlooked-for friends.

SOMERVILLE

 They are at hand, and you shall quickly know.
  Flourish. Enter below King Edward and Richard
  Duke of Gloucester, with Soldiers.

KING EDWARD

16 Go, trumpet, to the walls, and sound a parley.
  Sound a parley.

RICHARD DUKE OF GLOUCESTER

 See how the surly Warwick mans the wall.

WARWICK

18 O, unbid spite – is sportful Edward come?
 Where slept our scouts, or how are they seduced,
20 That we could hear no news of his repair?

KING EDWARD

 Now, Warwick, wilt thou ope the city gates,

---

6 *Da'ntry* i.e., Daventry (about 20 miles southeast of Coventry); *puissant* strong 9 *Southam* (about 10 miles southeast of Coventry) 12–13 *It . . . Warwick* (the city of Warwick lies southwest of Coventry; the earl has slightly mistaken directions, as Somerset points out) 14 *Belike* no doubt 16 *parley* trumpet call requesting a truce for conference 18 *unbid* uninvited, unwelcome; *sportful* lascivious 20 *repair* approach

Speak gentle words, and humbly bend thy knee,
Call Edward king, and at his hands beg mercy?
And he shall pardon thee these outrages.

WARWICK
Nay, rather, wilt thou draw thy forces hence,
Confess who set thee up and plucked thee down,
Call Warwick patron, and be penitent?
And thou shalt still remain the Duke of York.

RICHARD DUKE OF GLOUCESTER
I thought at least he would have said "the king."
Or did he make the jest against his will?   30

WARWICK
Is not a dukedom, sir, a goodly gift?

RICHARD DUKE OF GLOUCESTER
Ay, by my faith, for a poor earl to give.   32
I'll do thee service for so good a gift.   33

WARWICK
'Twas I that gave the kingdom to thy brother.

KING EDWARD
Why then, 'tis mine, if but by Warwick's gift.

WARWICK
Thou art no Atlas for so great a weight;   36
And, weakling, Warwick takes his gift again;
And Henry is my king, Warwick his subject.

KING EDWARD
But Warwick's king is Edward's prisoner,
And, gallant Warwick, do but answer this: 40
What is the body when the head is off?

RICHARD DUKE OF GLOUCESTER
Alas, that Warwick had no more forecast,   42
But whiles he thought to steal the single ten,   43
The king was slyly fingered from the deck.   44
    To Warwick

---

32 *poor earl* (a duke outranks an earl) 33 *do thee service* accept you as my
feudal overlord (ironically) 36 *Thou . . . for* i.e., you cannot bear (Atlas, a
Titan, supported the world on his shoulders) 42 *forecast* anticipated 43
single ten mere ten (the ten, highest of the plain cards, is worth having, but
not in comparison with the king) 44 *fingered* stolen

You left poor Henry at the bishop's palace,
And ten to one you'll meet him in the Tower.

KING EDWARD
'Tis even so – *(To Warwick)* yet you are Warwick still.

RICHARD DUKE OF GLOUCESTER
48   Come, Warwick, take the time – kneel down, kneel
     down.
49   Nay, when? Strike now, or else the iron cools.

WARWICK
50   I had rather chop this hand off at a blow,
     And with the other fling it at thy face,
52   Than bear so low a sail to strike to thee.

KING EDWARD
     Sail how thou canst, have wind and tide thy friend,
     This hand, fast wound about thy coal-black hair,
     Shall, whiles thy head is warm and new cut off,
     Write in the dust this sentence with thy blood:
57   "Wind-changing Warwick now can change no more."
          Enter the Earl of Oxford, with a Drummer and
          Soldiers bearing colors.

WARWICK
     O cheerful colors! See where Oxford comes.

OXFORD
     Oxford, Oxford, for Lancaster!
                              Oxford and his Men pass over the
                              stage and exeunt into the city.

RICHARD DUKE OF GLOUCESTER   *To King Edward*
60   The gates are open – let us enter too.

KING EDWARD
61   So other foes may set upon our backs?
     Stand we in good array, for they no doubt
63   Will issue out again and bid us battle.
     If not, the city being but of small defense,

---

48 *take the time* seize the opportunity   49 *Nay, when* (an exclamation indicating impatience)   52 *bear . . . sail* be so humble as (Warwick is punning
on Gloucester's use of *Strike* [=hit] in l. 49 with an allusion to sail-lowering
[=strike]; see the note to III.3.5)   57 *Wind-changing* i.e., fickle, inconstant;
s.d. *colors* flags   61 *So* so that   63 *bid* offer

We'll quickly rouse the traitors in the same.   65
WARWICK   *To Oxford, within*
O, welcome, Oxford – for we want thy help.   66
   Enter the Marquis of Montague, with a Drummer
   and Soldiers bearing colors.
MONTAGUE
Montague, Montague, for Lancaster!
            Montague and his Men pass over the stage
                           and exeunt into the city.
RICHARD DUKE OF GLOUCESTER
Thou and thy brother both shall bye this treason   68
Even with the dearest blood your bodies bear.
KING EDWARD
The harder matched, the greater victory.   70
My mind presageth happy gain and conquest.
   Enter the Duke of Somerset, with a Drummer and
   Soldiers bearing colors.
SOMERSET
Somerset, Somerset, for Lancaster!
            Somerset and his Men pass over the stage
                           and exeunt into the city.
RICHARD DUKE OF GLOUCESTER
Two of thy name, both Dukes of Somerset,   73
Have sold their lives unto the house of York –
And thou shalt be the third, an this sword hold.   75
   Enter George Duke of Clarence, with a Drummer and
   Soldiers bearing colors.
WARWICK
And lo, where George of Clarence sweeps along,
Of force enough to bid his brother battle;
With whom an upright zeal to right prevails   78

---

65 *rouse . . . in* drive . . . from (hunting terminology)   66 *want* need   68
bye atone for   73 *Two . . . name* (The Somerset being addressed is Edmund,
the fourth duke. His elder brother, Henry Beaufort, the third duke, was executed after the battle of Hexham, 1464, though his defection from Edward is
described in IV.1 and IV.2 as taking place in 1472. Their father, Edmund,
the second duke, was killed at Saint Albans, 1445; it is his head that Richard
throws down at I.1.20 s.d.)   75 *an* if   78 *to right* for justice

More than the nature of a brother's love.

GEORGE DUKE OF CLARENCE

80 Clarence, Clarence, for Lancaster!

KING EDWARD

81 *Et tu, Brutè* – wilt thou stab Caesar too?
To a Trumpeter

82 A parley, sirrah, to George of Clarence.
Sound a parley. Richard Duke of Gloucester and
George Duke of Clarence whisper together.

WARWICK

Come, Clarence, come – thou wilt if Warwick call.

GEORGE DUKE OF CLARENCE

Father of Warwick, know you what this means?
He takes his red rose out of his hat and throws it at
Warwick.

Look – here I throw my infamy at thee!
I will not ruinate my father's house,

87 Who gave his blood to lime the stones together,

88 And set up Lancaster. Why, trowest thou, Warwick,

89 That Clarence is so harsh, so blunt, unnatural,

90 To bend the fatal instruments of war
Against his brother and his lawful king?

92 Perhaps thou wilt object my holy oath.
To keep that oath were more impiety

94 Than Jephthah, when he sacrificed his daughter.
I am so sorry for my trespass made
That, to deserve well at my brothers' hands,
I here proclaim myself thy mortal foe,
With resolution, wheresoe'er I meet thee –

99 As I will meet thee, if thou stir abroad –

100 To plague thee for thy foul misleading me.
And so, proud-hearted Warwick, I defy thee,
And to my brothers turn my blushing cheeks.

---

81 *Et tu, Brutè* And you, too, Brutus? (Julius Caesar's exclamation when he realized that his friend was one of the conspirators to his murder) 82 *sirrah* fellow (said to a social inferior) 87 *lime* cement 88 *trowest thou* do you believe 89 *blunt* uncivilized 92 *object* raise as an objection 94 *Jephthah* (see Judges 11:30–40) 99 *abroad* i.e., outside Coventry

To King Edward
Pardon me, Edward – I will make amends.
   To Richard
And, Richard, do not frown upon my faults,
For I will henceforth be no more unconstant.   105

KING EDWARD
   Now welcome more, and ten times more beloved,
   Than if thou never hadst deserved our hate.

RICHARD DUKE OF GLOUCESTER   *To George*
   Welcome, good Clarence – this is brotherlike.

WARWICK   *To George*
   O, passing traitor – perjured and unjust!   109

KING EDWARD
   What, Warwick, wilt thou leave the town and fight?   *110*
   Or shall we beat the stones about thine ears?

WARWICK   *Aside*
   Alas, I am not cooped here for defense.   112
      To King Edward
   I will away towards Barnet presently,   113
   And bid thee battle, Edward, if thou dar'st.

KING EDWARD
   Yes, Warwick – Edward dares, and leads the way.
   Lords, to the field – Saint George and victory!
      Exeunt below King Edward and his company. March.
      The Earl of Warwick and his company descend and
      follow.

                          *

---

105 *unconstant* fickle **109** *passing* more than, unsurpassed **112** *cooped*
confined (i.e., prepared) **113** *Barnet* (about 10 miles north of London and
75 miles southeast of Coventry; by departing from the historical order of
events and having Henry captured in IV.10, Shakespeare is forced here to
treat Barnet as if it were adjacent to Coventry)

~ **V.2** *Alarum and excursions. Enter King Edward,*
bringing forth the Earl of Warwick, wounded.

KING EDWARD
    So lie thou there. Die thou, and die our fear –
2   For Warwick was a bug that feared us all.
    Now, Montague, sit fast – I seek for thee
    That Warwick's bones may keep thine company.   *Exit.*
WARWICK
    Ah, who is nigh? Come to me, friend or foe,
    And tell me who is victor, York or Warwick?
    Why ask I that? My mangled body shows,
    My blood, my want of strength, my sick heart shows,
    That I must yield my body to the earth
10 And by my fall the conquest to my foe.
11 Thus yields the cedar to the ax's edge,
12 Whose arms gave shelter to the princely eagle,
13 Under whose shade the ramping lion slept,
14 Whose top branch overpeered Jove's spreading tree
    And kept low shrubs from winter's powerful wind.
    These eyes, that now are dimmed with death's black
        veil,
    Have been as piercing as the midday sun
    To search the secret treasons of the world.
    The wrinkles in my brows, now filled with blood,
20 Were likened oft to kingly sepulchers –
    For who lived king, but I could dig his grave?
    And who durst smile when Warwick bent his brow?
    Lo now my glory smeared in dust and blood.
24 My parks, my walks, my manors that I had,
    Even now forsake me, and of all my lands

V.2 Near Barnet   2 *bug* goblin; *feared* frightened   11 *cedar* (symbol of pre-
eminence)   12–13 *eagle . . . lion* (the allusion may be general – i.e., "royal
creatures"; or it may be intended specifically, through the identification of
the men with their emblems – i.e., *eagle:* Richard of York, as perhaps at
II.1.91, and *lion:* Henry VI, three rampant lions being represented on his
royal arms)   13 *ramping* rampant   14 *overpeered* overlooked; *Jove's . . . tree*
i.e., the oak   24 *parks* hunting grounds

Is nothing left me but my body's length.
Why, what is pomp, rule, reign, but earth and dust?
And, live we how we can, yet die we must.
   Enter the Earl of Oxford and the Duke of Somerset.

SOMERSET
  Ah, Warwick, Warwick – wert thou as we are,
  We might recover all our loss again.   30
  The queen from France hath brought a puissant power. 31
  Even now we heard the news. Ah, couldst thou fly!

WARWICK
  Why, then I would not fly. Ah, Montague,
  If thou be there, sweet brother, take my hand,
  And with thy lips keep in my soul a while.   35
  Thou lov'st me not – for, brother, if thou didst,
  Thy tears would wash this cold congealèd blood
  That glues my lips and will not let me speak.
  Come quickly, Montague, or I am dead.

SOMERSET
  Ah, Warwick – Montague hath breathed his last,   40
  And to the latest gasp cried out for Warwick,   41
  And said, "Commend me to my valiant brother."
  And more he would have said, and more he spoke,
  Which sounded like a cannon in a vault,
  That mote not be distinguished; but at last   45
  I well might hear, delivered with a groan,
  "O, farewell, Warwick."

WARWICK
  Sweet rest his soul. Fly, lords, and save yourselves –
  For Warwick bids you all farewell, to meet in heaven.
    He dies.

OXFORD
  Away, away – to meet the queen's great power!   50
          Here they bear away Warwick's body. Exeunt.
                *

---

31 *puissant* strong; *power* army   **35** *with thy lips . . . a while* kiss me, and thereby briefly prolong my life (the soul was believed to escape through the mouth at death)   **41** *latest* final   **45** *mote* might

~ **V.3** *Flourish. Enter King Edward in triumph; with Richard Duke of Gloucester, George Duke of Clarence, and Soldiers.*

KING EDWARD
  Thus far our fortune keeps an upward course,
  And we are graced with wreaths of victory.
  But in the midst of this bright-shining day
  I spy a black suspicious threatening cloud
  That will encounter with our glorious sun
  Ere he attain his easeful western bed.
  I mean, my lords, those powers that the queen
8 Hath raised in Gallia have arrived our coast,
  And, as we hear, march on to fight with us.

GEORGE DUKE OF CLARENCE
10 A little gale will soon disperse that cloud,
  And blow it to the source from whence it came.
  Thy very beams will dry those vapors up,
13 For every cloud engenders not a storm.

RICHARD DUKE OF GLOUCESTER
14 The queen is valued thirty thousand strong,
  And Somerset, with Oxford, fled to her.
16 If she have time to breathe, be well assured,
  Her faction will be full as strong as ours.

KING EDWARD
18 We are advertised by our loving friends
19 That they do hold their course toward Tewkesbury.
20 We, having now the best at Barnet field,
21 Will thither straight, for willingness rids way –
  And, as we march, our strength will be augmented
  In every county as we go along.
  Strike up the drum, cry "Courage!" and away.
                       Flourish. March. Exeunt.

V.3 Near Barnet   **8** *Gallia* France   **13** *engenders* begets   **14** *The . . . valued* the queen's strength is thought to be   **16** *breathe* i.e., gather her strength   **18** *advertised* notified   **19** *Tewkesbury* a town in Gloucestershire   **20** *having . . . best* having now overcome   **21** *rids way* i.e., (seems to) decrease the distance

*

∿ **V.4** *Flourish. March. Enter Queen Margaret, Prince Edward, the Duke of Somerset, the Earl of Oxford, and Soldiers.*

QUEEN MARGARET
Great lords, wise men ne'er sit and wail their loss,
But cheerly seek how to redress their harms.   2
What though the mast be now blown overboard,
The cable broke, the holding anchor lost,
And half our sailors swallowed in the flood?
Yet lives our pilot still. Is't meet that he   6
Should leave the helm and, like a fearful lad,
With tearful eyes add water to the sea,
And give more strength to that which hath too much,
Whiles, in his moan, the ship splits on the rock   10
Which industry and courage might have saved?
Ah, what a shame; ah, what a fault were this.
Say Warwick was our anchor – what of that?
And Montague our topmast – what of him?
Our slaughtered friends the tackles – what of these?   15
Why, is not Oxford here another anchor?
And Somerset another goodly mast?
The friends of France our shrouds and tacklings?   18
And, though unskillful, why not Ned and I   19
For once allowed the skillful pilot's charge?   20
We will not from the helm to sit and weep,
But keep our course, though the rough wind say no,
From shelves and rocks that threaten us with wreck.   23
As good to chide the waves as speak them fair.

V.4 Fields near Tewkesbury 2 *cheerly* cheerfully 6 *our pilot* i.e., King Henry 10 *in* at; *moan* state of grief 15 *tackles* lines and pulleys for raising sail (running rigging) 18 *shrouds* lines bracing the mast (standing rigging); *tacklings* fittings and similar equipment 19 *Ned* Prince Edward (her son) 20 *charge* responsibility (i.e., to guide the ship) 23 *shelves* sandbanks; *wreck* ruin

And what is Edward but a ruthless sea?
What Clarence but a quicksand of deceit?
27   And Richard but a raggèd fatal rock?
28   All these the enemies to our poor bark.
Say you can swim – alas, 'tis but a while;
30   Tread on the sand – why, there you quickly sink;
Bestride the rock – the tide will wash you off,
Or else you famish. That's a threefold death.
This speak I, lords, to let you understand,
34   If case some one of you would fly from us,
That there's no hoped-for mercy with the brothers York
More than with ruthless waves, with sands, and rocks.
Why, courage then – what cannot be avoided
'Twere childish weakness to lament or fear.

PRINCE EDWARD
Methinks a woman of this valiant spirit
40   Should, if a coward heard her speak these words,
41   Infuse his breast with magnanimity
42   And make him, naked, foil a man at arms.
I speak not this as doubting any here –
For did I but suspect a fearful man,
45   He should have leave to go away betimes,
Lest in our need he might infect another
And make him of like spirit to himself.
If any such be here – as God forbid –
Let him depart before we need his help.

OXFORD
50   Women and children of so high a courage,
51   And warriors faint – why, 'twere perpetual shame!
52   O brave young prince, thy famous grandfather
Doth live again in thee! Long mayst thou live
To bear his image and renew his glories!

SOMERSET
And he that will not fight for such a hope,

---

27 *raggèd* jagged   28 *bark* ship   34 *If* in   41 *magnanimity* great courage
42 *naked* unarmed; *foil* defeat; *a man at arms* an armed man   45 *betimes* immediately   51 *faint* fainthearted   52 *grandfather* i.e., Henry V

Go home to bed, and like the owl by day,
If he arise, be mocked and wondered at.

QUEEN MARGARET
Thanks, gentle Somerset; sweet Oxford, thanks.

PRINCE EDWARD
And take his thanks that yet hath nothing else.   59
    Enter a Messenger.

MESSENGER
Prepare you, lords, for Edward is at hand   60
Ready to fight – therefore be resolute.

OXFORD
I thought no less. It is his policy
To haste thus fast to find us unprovided.   63

SOMERSET
But he's deceived; we are in readiness.

QUEEN MARGARET
This cheers my heart, to see your forwardness.   65

OXFORD
Here pitch our battle – hence we will not budge.   66
    Flourish and march. Enter King Edward, Richard
    Duke of Gloucester, and George Duke of Clarence,
    with Soldiers.

KING EDWARD   *To his followers*
Brave followers, yonder stands the thorny wood
Which, by the heavens' assistance and your strength,
Must by the roots be hewn up yet ere night.
I need not add more fuel to your fire,   70
For well I wot ye blaze to burn them out.   71
Give signal to the fight, and to it, lords.

QUEEN MARGARET   *To her followers*
Lords, knights, and gentlemen – what I should say
My tears gainsay; for every word I speak   74
Ye see I drink the water of my eye.
Therefore, no more but this: Henry your sovereign
Is prisoner to the foe, his state usurped,

---

59 *that yet* who as yet   63 *unprovided* unprepared   65 *forwardness* zeal   66
pitch our battle deploy our army   71 *wot* know   74 *gainsay* forbid

His realm a slaughterhouse, his subjects slain,
His statutes canceled, and his treasure spent –
80   And yonder is the wolf that makes this spoil.
You fight in justice; then in God's name, lords,
Be valiant, and give signal to the fight.
   Alarum, retreat, excursions.

                                          Exeunt.

                            *

⌀ **V.5** *Flourish. Enter King Edward, Richard Duke of*
   Gloucester, and George Duke of Clarence with Queen
   Margaret, the Earl of Oxford, and the Duke of
   Somerset, guarded.

KING EDWARD
1   Now here a period of tumultuous broils.
2   Away with Oxford to Hammes Castle straight;
For Somerset, off with his guilty head.
Go bear them hence – I will not hear them speak.
OXFORD
For my part, I'll not trouble thee with words.
                                    Exit, guarded.
SOMERSET
Nor I, but stoop with patience to my fortune.
                                    Exit, guarded.
QUEEN MARGARET
So part we sadly in this troublous world
8   To meet with joy in sweet Jerusalem.
KING EDWARD
Is proclamation made that who finds Edward
10   Shall have a high reward and he his life?
RICHARD DUKE OF GLOUCESTER
It is, and lo where youthful Edward comes.
   Enter Prince Edward, guarded.

_____

V.5 Fields near Tewkesbury 1 *period* full stop, end 2 *Hammes Castle* an
English fortification, southwest of Calais (where Oxford was confined after
his capture in 1474, three years later than Tewkesbury) 8 *Jerusalem* i.e.,
heaven, the New Jerusalem (Revelations 21:2)

KING EDWARD
  Bring forth the gallant – let us hear him speak.
  What, can so young a thorn begin to prick?
  Edward, what satisfaction canst thou make   14
  For bearing arms, for stirring up my subjects,
  And all the trouble thou hast turned me to?
PRINCE EDWARD
  Speak like a subject, proud ambitious York.
  Suppose that I am now my father's mouth –
  Resign thy chair, and where I stand, kneel thou,
  Whilst I propose the selfsame words to thee,   20
  Which, traitor, thou wouldst have me answer to.
QUEEN MARGARET
  Ah, that thy father had been so resolved.
RICHARD DUKE OF GLOUCESTER
  That you might still have worn the petticoat   23
  And ne'er have stolen the breech from Lancaster.   24
PRINCE EDWARD
  Let Aesop fable in a winter's night –   25
  His currish riddles sorts not with this place.   26
RICHARD DUKE OF GLOUCESTER
  By heaven, brat, I'll plague ye for that word.
QUEEN MARGARET
  Ay, thou wast born to be a plague to men.
RICHARD DUKE OF GLOUCESTER
  For God's sake take away this captive scold.
PRINCE EDWARD
  Nay, take away this scolding crookback rather.   30
KING EDWARD
  Peace, willful boy, or I will charm your tongue.   31

---

14 *satisfaction* recompense 23 *still* always 24 *breech* breeches (i.e., the
clothing of a man; literally, breeches are trousers that extend only just below
the knee) 25–26 *Let . . . place* i.e., you lie about the relationship between
my mother and father (with a gibe at Richard, for Aesop was supposedly
stunted and deformed) 26 *currish* mean, cynical; *sorts not* are not appropriate 30 *crookback* hunchback 31 *charm your tongue* i.e., silence you
(*charm:* cast a spell upon)

GEORGE DUKE OF CLARENCE   *To Prince Edward*
32   Untutored lad, thou art too malapert.
PRINCE EDWARD
        I know my duty – you are all undutiful.
        Lascivious Edward, and thou, perjured George,
        And thou, misshapen Dick – I tell ye all
        I am your better, traitors as ye are,
        And thou usurp'st my father's right and mine.
KING EDWARD
38   Take that, the likeness of this railer here.
            King Edward stabs Prince Edward.
RICHARD DUKE OF GLOUCESTER
39   Sprawl'st thou? Take that, to end thy agony.
            Richard stabs Prince Edward.
GEORGE DUKE OF CLARENCE
40   And there's for twitting me with perjury.
            George stabs Prince Edward, who dies.
QUEEN MARGARET
41   O, kill me too!
RICHARD DUKE OF GLOUCESTER
                        Marry, and shall.
            He offers to kill her.
KING EDWARD
        Hold, Richard, hold – for we have done too much.
RICHARD DUKE OF GLOUCESTER
        Why should she live to fill the world with words?
            Queen Margaret faints.
KING EDWARD
        What – doth she swoon? Use means for her recovery.
RICHARD DUKE OF GLOUCESTER   *Aside to George*
        Clarence, excuse me to the king my brother.
        I'll hence to London on a serious matter.
47   Ere ye come there, be sure to hear some news.

---

32 *malapert* impertinent   38 *railer* scold (i.e., Queen Margaret)   39 *Sprawl'st thou?* Do you struggle in your death throes?   41 *Marry, and shall* I will indeed (*marry*: by the Virgin Mary, a mild oath)   41 s.d. *offers* threatens   47 *Ere* before; *be sure to* be confident that you will

GEORGE DUKE OF CLARENCE   *Aside to Richard*
  What? What?
RICHARD DUKE OF GLOUCESTER   *Aside to George*
  The Tower, the Tower.   *Exit.*
QUEEN MARGARET
  O Ned, sweet Ned – speak to thy mother, boy.   50
  Canst thou not speak? O traitors, murderers!
  They that stabbed Caesar shed no blood at all,
  Did not offend, nor were not worthy blame,
  If this foul deed were by to equal it.   54
  He was a man – this, in respect, a child;   55
  And men ne'er spend their fury on a child.
  What's worse than murderer that I may name it?
  No, no, my heart will burst an if I speak;
  And I will speak that so my heart may burst.
  Butchers and villains! Bloody cannibals!   60
  How sweet a plant have you untimely cropped!
  You have no children, butchers; if you had,
  The thought of them would have stirred up remorse.
  But if you ever chance to have a child,
  Look in his youth to have him so cut off
  As, deathsmen, you have rid this sweet young prince!   66
KING EDWARD
  Away with her – go, bear her hence perforce.
QUEEN MARGARET
  Nay, never bear me hence – dispatch me here.   68
  Here sheathe thy sword – I'll pardon thee my death.
  What? Wilt thou not? Then, Clarence, do it thou.   70
GEORGE DUKE OF CLARENCE
  By heaven, I will not do thee so much ease.
QUEEN MARGARET
  Good Clarence, do; sweet Clarence, do thou do it.
GEORGE DUKE OF CLARENCE
  Didst thou not hear me swear I would not do it?

---

54 *by* nearby; *equal* compare with   55 *in respect* by comparison   66 *rid*
killed   68 *dispatch* kill

QUEEN MARGARET

74   Ay, but thou usest to forswear thyself.
      'Twas sin before, but now 'tis charity.
      What, wilt thou not? Where is that devil's butcher,
77   Hard-favored Richard? Richard, where art thou?
78   Thou art not here. Murder is thy alms deed –
79   Petitioners for blood thou ne'er putt'st back.

KING EDWARD

80   Away, I say – I charge ye, bear her hence.

QUEEN MARGARET

      So come to you and yours as to this prince!

                                                    Exit, guarded.

KING EDWARD

      Where's Richard gone?

GEORGE DUKE OF CLARENCE

83   To London all in post – *(Aside)* and as I guess,
      To make a bloody supper in the Tower.

KING EDWARD

      He's sudden if a thing comes in his head.
86   Now march we hence. Discharge the common sort
      With pay and thanks, and let's away to London,
      And see our gentle queen how well she fares.
89   By this I hope she hath a son for me.   *Exeunt.*

                            *

∽ **V.6** *Enter, on the walls, King Henry the Sixth,
      reading a book, Richard Duke of Gloucester,
      and the Lieutenant of the Tower.*

RICHARD DUKE OF GLOUCESTER

1   Good day, my lord. What, at your book so hard?

KING HENRY

      Ay, my good lord – "my lord," I should say, rather.

---

74 *thou . . . to forswear* you have the habit of forswearing   77 *Hard-favored*
ugly   78 *alms deed* act of charity   79 *Petitioners . . . back* you never turn
away those who ask for blood   83 *post* haste   86 *common sort* ordinary soldiers   89 *this* this time
V.6 The Tower, London   1 *book* (of devotions)

'Tis sin to flatter; "good" was little better.   3
"Good Gloucester" and "good devil" were alike,
And both preposterous – therefore not "good lord."   5

RICHARD DUKE OF GLOUCESTER   *To the Lieutenant*
Sirrah, leave us to ourselves. We must confer.   6

Exit Lieutenant.

KING HENRY
So flies the reckless shepherd from the wolf;   7
So first the harmless sheep doth yield his fleece,
And next his throat unto the butcher's knife.
What scene of death hath Roscius now to act?   10

RICHARD DUKE OF GLOUCESTER
Suspicion always haunts the guilty mind;
The thief doth fear each bush an officer.

KING HENRY
The bird that hath been limèd in a bush   13
With trembling wings misdoubteth every bush.   14
And I, the hapless male to one sweet bird,   15
Have now the fatal object in my eye
Where my poor young was limed, was caught and
killed.

RICHARD DUKE OF GLOUCESTER
Why, what a peevish fool was that of Crete,   18
That taught his son the office of a fowl!
And yet, for all his wings, the fool was drowned.   20

KING HENRY
I, Daedalus; my poor boy, Icarus;
Thy father, Minos, that denied our course;
The sun that seared the wings of my sweet boy,   23

---

3 *better* i.e., better than flattery   5 *preposterous* unnatural   6 *Sirrah* fellow
(used of a social inferior)   7 *reckless* heedless   10 *Roscius* a famous Roman
actor (died 62 BC), supposed by the Elizabethans to be the greatest of all
tragedians   13 *limèd* caught with birdlime   14 *misdoubteth* suspects   15
hapless unlucky; *male* father; *bird* chick   18 *peevish* ridiculous   18–25
fool . . . life (Daedalus wished to escape from Crete, having been imprisoned
there by King Minos. He devised wings for himself and his son Icarus, fas-
tening them on with wax. The father flew to safety, but Icarus rose too near
the sun, the heat melted the wax, and he fell into the sea and was drowned.)
23–24 *sun . . . Edward* (referring to the sun insignia of York)

Thy brother Edward; and thyself, the sea,
25 Whose envious gulf did swallow up his life.
Ah, kill me with thy weapon, not with words!
27 My breast can better brook thy dagger's point
Than can my ears that tragic history.
But wherefore dost thou come? Is't for my life?

RICHARD DUKE OF GLOUCESTER
30 Think'st thou I am an executioner?

KING HENRY
A persecutor I am sure thou art;
If murdering innocents be executing,
Why, then thou art an executioner.

RICHARD DUKE OF GLOUCESTER
Thy son I killed for his presumption.

KING HENRY
Hadst thou been killed when first thou didst presume,
Thou hadst not lived to kill a son of mine.
And thus I prophesy: that many a thousand
38 Which now mistrust no parcel of my fear,
And many an old man's sigh, and many a widow's,
40 And many an orphan's water-standing eye –
Men for their sons', wives for their husbands',
42 Orphans for their parents' timeless death –
Shall rue the hour that ever thou wast born.
The owl shrieked at thy birth – an evil sign;
45 The night crow cried, aboding luckless time;
Dogs howled, and hideous tempests shook down trees;
47 The raven rooked her on the chimney's top;
48 And chatt'ring pies in dismal discords sung.
Thy mother felt more than a mother's pain,
50 And yet brought forth less than a mother's hope –
51 To wit, an indigested and deformèd lump,
Not like the fruit of such a goodly tree.

---

25 *envious gulf* hateful gullet 27 *brook* endure 38 *mistrust no parcel* do not
suspect any part 40 *water-standing* full of tears 42 *timeless* untimely 45
night crow bird of evil omen; *aboding* foreboding 47 *rooked her* squatted
48 *pies* magpies 51 *indigested* shapeless

Teeth hadst thou in thy head when thou wast born,
To signify thou cam'st to bite the world;
And if the rest be true which I have heard,
Thou cam'st –

RICHARD DUKE OF GLOUCESTER
I'll hear no more. Die, prophet, in thy speech.
He stabs him.
For this, amongst the rest, was I ordained.

KING HENRY
Ay, and for much more slaughter after this.
O, God forgive my sins, and pardon thee.   60
He dies.

RICHARD DUKE OF GLOUCESTER
What – will the aspiring blood of Lancaster
Sink in the ground? I thought it would have mounted.
See how my sword weeps for the poor king's death.
O, may such purple tears be alway shed   64
From those that wish the downfall of our house!
If any spark of life be yet remaining,
Down, down to hell, and say I sent thee thither –
He stabs him again.
I that have neither pity, love, nor fear.
Indeed, 'tis true that Henry told me of,
For I have often heard my mother say   70
I came into the world with my legs forward.
Had I not reason, think ye, to make haste,
And seek their ruin that usurped our right?
The midwife wondered and the women cried,
"O, Jesus bless us, he is born with teeth!" –
And so I was, which plainly signified
That I should snarl and bite and play the dog.
Then, since the heavens have shaped my body so,
Let hell make crooked my mind to answer it.   79
I had no father, I am like no father;   80
I have no brother, I am like no brother;
And this word "love," which graybeards call divine,

---

64 *purple* i.e., bloody   79 *answer* accord with

Be resident in men like one another
And not in me – I am myself alone.
Clarence, beware; thou kept'st me from the light –
86 But I will sort a pitchy day for thee.
87 For I will buzz abroad such prophecies
That Edward shall be fearful of his life,
And then, to purge his fear, I'll be thy death.
90 Henry and his son are gone; thou, Clarence, art next;
And by one and one I will dispatch the rest,
Counting myself but bad till I be best.
I'll throw thy body in another room
And triumph, Henry, in thy day of doom.

Exit with the body.

*

∾ **V.7** *A chair of state. Flourish. Enter King Edward,
Queen Elizabeth, George Duke of Clarence, Richard
Duke of Gloucester, the Lord Hastings, a Nurse
carrying the infant Prince Edward, and Attendants.*

KING EDWARD
Once more we sit in England's royal throne,
Repurchased with the blood of enemies.
3 What valiant foemen, like to autumn's corn,
4 Have we mowed down in tops of all their pride!
Three dukes of Somerset, threefold renowned
6 For hardy and undoubted champions;
7 Two Cliffords, as the father and the son;
And two Northumberlands – two braver men
9 Ne'er spurred their coursers at the trumpet's sound.
10 With them, the two brave bears, Warwick and Montague,
That in their chains fettered the kingly lion

---

86 *sort* seek out (as being befitting); *pitchy* black   87 *buzz* whisper (scandal)
    V.7 The palace, London   3 *corn* wheat   4 *in tops* at the peak   6 *un-
doubted* fearless   7 *as* to wit   9 *coursers* warhorses   10 *bears* (a bear chained
to a staff was the emblem of the Neville family, which included the brothers
Warwick and Montague)

And made the forest tremble when they roared.
Thus have we swept suspicion from our seat   13
And made our footstool of security.
  To Queen Elizabeth
Come hither, Bess, and let me kiss my boy.
  The Nurse brings forth the infant prince. King
  Edward kisses him.
Young Ned, for thee, thine uncles and myself
Have in our armors watched the winter's night,   17
Went all afoot in summer's scalding heat,
That thou mightst repossess the crown in peace;
And of our labors thou shalt reap the gain.   20

RICHARD DUKE OF GLOUCESTER   *Aside*
  I'll blast his harvest, an your head were laid;   21
  For yet I am not looked on in the world.   22
  This shoulder was ordained so thick to heave;
  And heave it shall some weight or break my back.
  Work thou the way, and thou shalt execute.   25

KING EDWARD
  Clarence and Gloucester, love my lovely queen;
  And kiss your princely nephew, brothers, both.

GEORGE DUKE OF CLARENCE
  The duty that I owe unto your majesty
  I seal upon the lips of this sweet babe.   29
    He kisses the infant prince.

QUEEN ELIZABETH
  Thanks, noble Clarence – worthy brother, thanks.   30

RICHARD DUKE OF GLOUCESTER
  And that I love the tree from whence thou sprang'st,   31
  Witness the loving kiss I give the fruit.
    He kisses the infant prince.
    Aside
  To say the truth, so Judas kissed his master,

---

13 *suspicion* apprehension; *seat* throne   17 *watched* stayed awake during
21 *blast* wither; *an* if; *laid* laid down (dead)   22 *looked on* respected   25
thou . . . thou (he indicates first his head and then his arm or shoulder)   29
seal pledge   31 *tree* i.e., the family of York

34   And cried "All hail!" whenas he meant all harm.

KING EDWARD

Now am I seated as my soul delights,

Having my country's peace and brothers' loves.

GEORGE DUKE OF CLARENCE

What will your grace have done with Margaret?

René her father, to the King of France

39   Hath pawned the Sicils and Jerusalem,

40   And hither have they sent it for her ransom.

KING EDWARD

41   Away with her, and waft her hence to France.

42   And now what rests but that we spend the time

43   With stately triumphs, mirthful comic shows,

Such as befits the pleasure of the court?

45   Sound drums and trumpets – farewell, sour annoy!

For here, I hope, begins our lasting joy.

Flourish. Exeunt.

---

34 *whenas* when   39 *the Sicils* Naples and Sicily   40 *it* i.e., the money raised
41 *waft* transport across water   42 *rests* remains (to be done)   43 *triumphs*
festivities   45 *sour annoy* bitter tribulation